RICK STEIN'S
MEDITERRANEAN ESCAPES

To Sarah, Zach and Olivia with love

Food photography by Earl Carter

Food styling by Debbie Major

Location photography by Craig Easton

This book is published to accompany the television series entitled *Rick Stein's Mediterranean Escapes,* first broadcast on BBC2 in 2007.

The series was produced for BBC Television by Denham Productions

Producer and director: David Pritchard

Assistant producer: Arezoo Farahzad

Executive producer for the BBC: Tom Archer

10 9 8 7

Published in 2007 by BBC Books, an imprint of Ebury Publishing.

A Random House Group Company.

The Random House Group Limited Reg. No. 954009

Addresses for companies within the Random House Group can be found at **www.randomhouse.co.uk**

A CIP catalogue record for this book is available from the British Library.

ISBN 978 0 563 49366 2

The Random House Group Limited makes every effort to ensure that the papers used in our books are made from trees that have been legally sourced from well-managed and credibly certified forests. Our paper procurement policy can be found at **www.randomhouse.co.uk**

To buy books by your favourite authors and register for offers visit **www.rbooks.co.uk**

Commissioning editors: Vivien Bowler and Nicky Ross

Project editor: Mari Roberts

Designer: Lisa Pettibone

Assistant food stylist: Mandy Biffin

Map illustration: Joy Gosney

Production controller: Ken McKay

Colour origination: GRB Editrice Ltd

Printed and bound in Germany by Firmengruppe APPL, Wemding

Background image: Cap Corse peninsula, Corsica

RICK STEIN'S
MEDITERRANEAN ESCAPES

CONTENTS

ACKNOWLEDGEMENTS

I WOULD LIKE TO THANK Debbie Major, with whom I've worked over the last twelve years producing nine books. There is no doubt that this book would never have been finished without her persistence and dedication. She has done the lion's share of the hard work, both in writing up and testing the recipes and in cooking the food, not only for the food photography, but also getting me up to speed with the food filming. I would also like to thank my commissioning editor, Nicky Ross; it is the first time I have worked with her, but it has proven to be a felicitous partnership. I would also like to mention my former editor Viv Bowler, who set the whole project up and was responsible for the original format. This is the first, I hope, of many photographic projects with Earl Carter. Debbie and I travelled to Australia in February 2007 to work with him at a time when the summer light and produce were more vibrant, reflecting the sort of food and surroundings that I encountered in the Mediterranean. Yet again, and for a number of my previous books, I would like to thank Craig Easton for his evocative landscape photography throughout the book and for the brilliant cover. The design of the book is totally new in concept and for this I would like to thank Lisa Pettibone. And once again too, thank you to my page editor Mari Roberts for her patience and good old-fashioned knowledge of grammar, spelling and meaning of words. It goes without saying that the TV series *Rick Stein's Mediterranean Escapes* which accompanies this book has provided culinary experiences, excitement and a deep sense of participating in something quite special, and for this I would like to thank my chum and Producer/Director David Pritchard, Assistant Producer Arezoo Farahzad, Cameraman Chris Topliss, Sound Engineer Pete Underwood and also stand-in Cameraman Jean Pierre Newman, who covered for Chris when he was laid up with something nasty he caught in Morocco.

The research team deserves credit too. Bernard Hall for his invaluable reminders about literary figures, painters and musicians who crop up everywhere in the Mediterranean, Adam Kennedy who took me to a valley in Morocco to hear my first nightingale at dusk, and the tireless Debbie Major again, who did the research for both Turkey and Morocco and introduced me to many of the new ingredients and dishes of these countries. I would then like to thank for all their help while I was abroad: Val Sykes in Corsica; Anna Maggio in Sardinia, Sicily and Puglia; Dominique Carroll and Anna Skidmore in Mallorca; Xosé Ferreres, Sandra Labenne and Norbert Fusté in Catalonia, Spain; Hilary Paipeti in Corfu; Serhan Gungor, Filiz Hosukoglu and Turker Keser, our driver, in Turkey; and Saad Abbassi, Tim Buxton, Karima Elbakkouchi and Hicham Ouahabi, our driver, in Morocco.

And I'd also like to mention for their help during the food photography in Australia: Michele Finato for such wonderful props; Mandy Biffin for assisting Debbie and for allowing us to use her beautiful home for some of the photography; Geoff Lung for the hire of his studio, and all his team for great coffee; and Valli Little for all her help and advice.

Back at home, I would like to say a word of thanks to numerous people for their help and support: Matthew Stevens, our fish merchant, and his team, for providing us with superb fish and seafood for the recipe testing and filming; David West of Sway Butchers, one of the best butchers around; Dominique Carroll and the tourist office of Mallorca for an express delivery of sobrasada; Odysea for supplying us with superb authentic Greek cheeses; Claire Heron-Maxwell for all her help during food filming; and Robert Entwistle of Thomas and Thomas, for making my beautiful handmade kitchen and the bespoke central island on which I cooked during filming.

And last, my PA Viv Taylor, who was very fair in dividing my time between filming, book writing, running the restaurants and trips to be with Sarah in Australia. And thanks to my sons, Edward, Jack and Charles, who tried many of these dishes when I cooked them round at the cottage for dinner, and commented favourably on everything, except sobrasada.

ESCAPE ROUTES

A COUPLE OF YEARS AGO, I made a TV series about a barge journey down the canals of France from Bordeaux to Marseille. In the last episode, we finally made it to the Mediterranean, not quite at Marseille but at the mouth of the Rhône at Port St-Louis. We took the old river barge, the Anjodi, right out to sea, and my overriding thought, because I love filming so much, and because the food in the Languedoc and Provence was so sunny and warm, and because I was filled with such a sense of well-being, was: let's keep going! We had been on the boat for about eight weeks and had to get back and get on with the rest of our lives, but I think all of us were charmed by the thought that before long we'd start again, where we left off.

So it was that I found myself on the SNCM *Napoleon Bonaparte* on my way from Marseille to Bastia in Corsica for the first part of a journey to discover the Mediterranean. It had to be by ferry because I was driving a Land Rover, but it's a great way to travel. You leave Marseille in the early evening, and by the time the old houses on the quay in Bastia come into view, just as dawn is breaking, you're thinking about Napoleon, the maquis, chestnuts, the thick red wine, ewe's milk cheese, figatellu and smoky mountain ham. I had been reading Paul Theroux's *The Pillars of Hercules* on the way over, or rather trying to, but Prudence, David the director's dog, had been 'reading' it back in Devon, so the cover and quite a lot of the pages had been converted to papier-mâché by the dribble and giant teeth of a bull terrier. But before turning in, with the sea swishing below my porthole, I did read about 'the haunted quality of the island and its vigorous language, the sweet aroma of its maquis, the fatuity of its cult of Napoleon'. It made the start of a new journey even more exciting.

Next morning I only just made it to the bow for a camera chat celebrating the ferry's arrival in Bastia. I was rushing around the cabin panicking, mobile ringing, with David saying, 'Where are you, be quick, or we'll be there.' I slammed the door and ran down the narrow corridor with cabins of sleeping passengers on either side, dragging my case, then saw that I had forgotten my phone. Surely not, it's my lifeline. Back in the cabin I found it on the porthole sill. How could I do that? I was certain I'd checked everything. I'll never be a proper traveller. I scrambled on to the deck and was immediately captivated by the oil-painting view in front, the old houses on the quay in the golden light of early morning. I only found out later that David had persuaded the captain to slow the boat down to give me time to get up there before we docked.

The first day's filming in a new country tends to make me nervous. We were on our way to a Corsican chef's cookery school to film him roasting kid with fresh cocos roses beans. Would he be difficult and arrogant and French, I worried. I wasn't much calmed by the sight of the place: a very old stone house with a tower. Style, serious cookery, a sense of history, this was going to be a hard morning of struggling with the language and smothering a rising irritation at the French, who know best when it comes to cooking. But I soon realized that this was Corsica, not France, and Vincent Tabarani was remarkably modest and friendly. It was a quick lesson in rugged Corsican upland food, its good meat, smoked mountain ham, chestnuts, wild mushrooms, pungent cheeses – all raw materials of the best quality.

His students were all local. We sat outside looking through Corsican pines down to the calm blue Mediterranean, eating roasted kid with figs, tomatoes and those lovely cocos roses, which we know as borlotti beans, and drinking more red Patrimonio, and I had an intense feeling of happiness at being on another expedition.

I wouldn't like to have you believe that every expedition was perfection. We drove to a mountain village called Sorio to film a feast in a converted church. I assumed I was going to meet some hardy Corsicans who had lived in this high, sunny hamlet for ever. However, the majority of the population appeared to be retired civil servants and schoolteachers from Lyon and Marseille. The feast started with

South coast of Corsica from Bonifacio

pulenda. It's a chestnut flour accompaniment to meat. I thought it was awful: sickly sweet, sticky, soft and entirely unsatisfying to the palate. I had had romantic notions that I was in the process of finding the new polenta. They make much of the ceremony of heating and stirring the chestnut flour with water until it thickens, then pouring it out onto a table, where it sets into a floppy cake, which they then cut into slices. Everyone gets some to eat with their grilled figatellu, the smoked liver and pork sausage they were cooking over wood embers in the fireplace of the village hall. But when they started sending round the figatellu, hot with the scent of wood smoke, sandwiched into some really excellent freshly baked bread, with slices of ewe's milk cheese, I finally began to smile. The hot fat from the sausages soaked into the bread in a thoroughly satisfying way, and then the singing started. They were folk songs by a local ensemble, the sound plaintive and haunting, and some of their faces strangely hard to categorize, particularly one man in his early fifties, in a tight suit with short black hair plastered neatly to his head with brilliantine, who looked like Picasso.

The Corsicans look rugged; they fit the terrain. We filmed a shepherd called Jean François milking his sheep on a chilly morning in his shack up in the hills near the almost medieval village of Lama high above the Ostriconi valley. Later we went back to his tiny fromagerie in the village and watched his wife making their ewe's milk cheese. These mountain village cheeses are beautifully sharp and delicate. He explained that their fragrance came from the sheep's diet of maquis herbs such as bush myrtle, many kinds of mint including nepeta (catmint), rosemary, thyme and oregano.

One thing I found surprising: you don't find much fish on the island. To enjoy the food of Corsica, you need to love wild boar, smoked sausage, lamb, goat's cheese and ham, and fantastic distant views of mountain tops, pines and rocks with the glinting blue sea in the background.

I was thinking about this as I was leaving Bonifacio on a short and extremely turbulent ferry journey to Santa Teresa Gallura in Sardinia. For all its beauty, Corsica has a slightly sombre feel. Not so Sardinia. It was early May and glorious – it felt like we were the first tourists ever to go there. Ridiculous, of course, but that's one of the pleasures of going on food travels: you tend to head for places that are out of the tourist way. I'm thinking in particular of two places, Cabras on the west coast and Oliena in the centre. We went to Cabras to see an old method of fishing for grey mullet. Reed and cane traps are laid right across the river and the fish are guided into a chamber where they are caught in big nets. We must have seen half a ton of fish scooped out into boxes. It's sold locally and the roe is salted and dried and made into bottarga. What struck me, apart from the visual appeal of this estuary with the incredibly intricate and attractive walls of cane and reeds, was the demeanour of the fishermen. The food writer Marcella Hazan writes about the Italians' inexhaustible facility for making art out of life, and here it was, in action. These guys were macho. They smoked nonchalantly while they worked, shouting and strutting about, fit and healthy and full of beans. Later at lunch we ate at a busy restaurant in Cabras called Il Caminetto, where they served the mullet poached in water and then wrapped in sea purslane. It's left to cool and then served cold, by which time it has taken on some of the flavour of the purslane. I crave it even now.

We had gone to Oliena to visit an agriturismo, just outside the town, to watch Costantino Puggioni cook suckling pig over an open fire. He threw whole bay leaf branches and other herbs onto the flames so that the smoke permeated the meat. He took a large lump of lardo (cured pork back fat), lit it in the fire and basted the carcasses with the flaming fat. The skin of the pig was imbued with herbed smoke and delicately crisp. That was my lasting memory of Sardinia. It's a beautiful island, even if some of the inland towns are a bit thrown together. Although there are mountainous parts, like Corsica, unlike that island there's much more pastoral countryside and a lot of excellent beaches.

On the ferry into Trapani on Sicily, I got a message on my phone saying welcome to Tunisia: that's how close North Africa is. There is plenty of culinary evidence of influences from across the water – fish couscous and pine nuts and currants in savoury dishes – but Sicily is also everything that everybody loves about Italy, only more so. It's beautiful; there are miles of unspoilt, deeply attractive countryside; it has

wonderful food, great cities and, for the tourists at least, excitement, thanks to an ever-present though illusory sense of danger. The number of times people have said to me, 'Is it safe?' and I have replied, in a well-heeled-traveller sort of way and with a great sense of satisfaction, 'Oh, not too bad,' are many.

Palermo is stuffed with ornately decorated 18th-century houses, palaces and churches, most of them gently falling down. The sense of romantic decay is everywhere. We stayed at the seaside suburb of Mondello, where many mafia bosses have their villas, and ate octopus, calamari and swordfish. We went out fishing with a giant of a man who recalled the Mediterranean in the 1960s. He said, 'Then, there was plenty of fish but no one had money. Now there's plenty of money, largely through drug trafficking, but no fish.' La Vucciria market in the centre of the city was delightful. I ate tiny snails, gathered from wild fennel stalks, with olive oil, garlic and parsley, and marvelled at the extensive selection of poached bull's penises at a nearby deli counter.

The market in Catania was similarly exciting, the theatricality of Italians so endearing. Everyone was shouting, cajoling, demanding while selling their wares, particularly the swordfish and tuna sellers with massive slices of red and translucent marble-white fish. There was a shellfish stall selling sea urchins, mussels and clams, and something I'd never seen on sale before: limpets. These, they explained, I had to eat raw with lemon juice, which I did. There was one counter with a display strewn over crushed ice: small red mullet, silver bream and bass, sardines and green seaweed, all apparently at random and looking rather like a Jackson Pollock painting. We found a fish restaurant on the side of the market where we ate tiny prawns dredged in flour and deep-fried, grilled swordfish with salmoriglio and spaghetti vongole. I've included some of my thoughts about Sicily in the introductions to the recipes, but as a cook what I like about the Sicilians is their absolute loyalty to the quality of raw materials. Someone once said, 'In France food is all about the genius of cooks; in Italy it's about the glory of God.'

My next trip was towards the end of June, to Mallorca. I first went there in the early 1960s with a friend from school, the first trip I had taken without my family anywhere. I worked in a little breakfast bar in Cala Mayor just outside Palma, frying eggs and chips in olive oil. I loved it. But I wasn't looking forward to going back. It is much more built up in the south now, but get away from the Palma area – which is

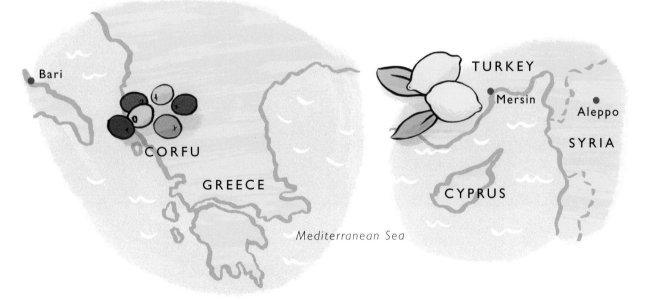

Porto Colom, Mallorca

actually a lovely city with old houses with first-floor bay windows, a beautiful cathedral dominating the harbour and great shops – and you enter another world. They've come to terms with the enormous economic benefits of tourism, along with its downside of endless cafes selling British beer and pizzas, by opening up the centre to people who want to understand what rural Mallorca is like. I was taken by our guide, Dominique Carroll, to a mountain restaurant called Es Verger, just below the Castell d'Alaró. After a splendid lunch of wood-fire-roasted lamb, we hiked up to the precipitous castle with a large number of German walkers. No tourists on the island in the 1960s would have been aware of this glorious landscape of mountains and valleys.

I was extremely surprised at how good the food was. Most of the population came across from Catalonia when the Moors were bloodily ejected in the 14th century, so although many dishes are similar to those in Spain, others, particularly those built around sobrasada (pork and pimentón sausage), are very much local. Dishes like the chicken with sobrasada on page 115, pasta and even various fish dishes are made distinctive by it. I must also mention pa amb oli: bread with oil. Tomás Graves has written a whole book on the subject and indeed has a rock band of the same name. We met him at a restaurant famous for pa amb oli, Bar S'Hostal at Montuiri. Like good rock and roll, he says, it's easy to get simple things wrong, and he couldn't stress enough the importance of this simple idea to Mallorcan culture. He took a big slice of fairly stale, rustic bread, grated a juicy tomato onto it and sprinkled it with olive oil and salt. I liked Tomás. He was a worrier, particularly on the modern diet of the islanders. 'Even the gypsies are getting fat,' he said.

I went to Deia, where his father, Robert Graves, had lived for over fifty years. Gertrude Stein had advised him that Mallorca is 'paradise – if you can stand it'. The town and all the west coast of Mallorca is indeed that, with mountains coming dramatically down to the sea. Robert Graves's house on the road into town was rather disappointing, though. It was being renovated into a museum of his work. I suppose I expected a place in the hills: old, almost Andalucian, with white walls and an internal courtyard – so intense have my romantic thoughts of his life there, surrounded by writers, artists and colourful people, been over the years since I read *Good-bye To All That*. The goodbye was his leaving of England for Mallorca. On my way through the Mediterranean I kept bumping into the reputations of authors in self-exile from their homes, normally in northern Europe, and thought with some humour about how unlikely it was that any of the locals had read their work. On the way to Andratx, on an incredibly winding road from the hills down to the bay below, was a restaurant where I had some of the best gambas (rosy-pink

Palma fish market, Mallorca

Bosa Marina, Sardinia

prawns) cooked with sea salt that I have ever eaten, cabracho con cebolla (rascasse/scorpion fish with onions), and a great rice and fish soup with allioli. I'm not going to tell you where it is – you'll have to work it out for yourself.

Catalonia was my first trip to any part of the mainland around the Mediterranean. I headed straight for the Boqueria market in Barcelona, the market by which all others could be judged. I've written about it in recipes on pages 25 and 90, but I noticed on the internet someone describing it as like 'going through heaven's doors'. I think it's something about the beauty of the building itself. It has an ornate entrance doorway, with a colourful hanging crest at the top of it saying 'Mercat St Josep La Boqueria', and a glass roof. Its elegance inspires the stallholders to outdo each other in colourful and elaborate displays of their produce.

This is my homage to Catalonia: cooking and eating a fish stew on a boat with a group of local fishermen in Sant Carles de la Ràpita. I must confess that I arrived convinced they had agreed to stage a pretend-cooking-of-the-fish sequence for the tourists, but this was no pretence. I still marvel at the simplicity of the ingredients the fisherman, Mayan, used to cook a dish of mullet and gilthead bream: olive oil, tomato, garlic and potato. He took a big aluminium pan and put it on a tiny stove in his wheelhouse, threw in some oil, three or four cloves of garlic, just one large tomato, roughly chopped up, and some really waxy peeled potatoes, then added the fish, covered everything in water, added salt and brought it to the boil. At the stern of the boat two others were busy making allioli in a bright yellow mortar with a wooden pestle. As soon as the fish and potatoes were cooked, Mayan poured off three-quarters of the broth and brought the pan through for us to devour with the allioli, some local crusty bread and a very simple cold white wine. I'm feeling quite emotional while I'm writing this: maybe it was the pungency of the allioli, the sweetness of the potatoes or tomatoes, the freshness of the fish, or the prosaic location on the stern of the boat under an awning to keep off the hot sun, but it was absolutely unforgettable. And then there was more. He got a shallow, round, battered aluminium pan, poured in some oil, threw in a few slices of garlic and a cup or two of bomba rice, some salt and the rest of the broth, brought it all to a boil and left it to simmer. He cooked it until it was dry but all the grains of rice were swollen with the fish broth, and he brought it through and we ate it with the remaining allioli. I feel very privileged to have been there.

We next surfaced, after a lengthy trip back to Britain, in Puglia, right down south on the heel of Italy. A friend of mine with a house in Tuscany said she didn't care for it much. The towns of Brindisi, Bari and Lecce are surrounded by heavy industry, and everywhere is pretty flat and dusty. I think she described it as scruffy.

Northern Corfu

One of my growing realizations about the Mediterranean was that scruffy is good. The Mediterranean coast of Spain used to be scruffy; Sant Carles de la Ràpita still is, but most of that coast is now big hotels and concrete. Puglia is where the local Italians go to spend their holidays and it has a comfortable, scruffy feeling about it. I remember a sea urchin (*riccio di mare*) restaurant on the flat coast by the flat sea over an Easter Monday: just a couple of wooden sheds and an old caravan with awnings everywhere, but there must have been three hundred Italians having lunch there, eating raw sea-urchin roes into which you dipped fresh bread or ate with tiny plastic spoons, or else you ordered pasta with *ricci*, a big bowl of *al dente* spaghetti with olive oil, garlic, chilli, parsley and sea urchins stirred in at the last minute. It's a real pleasure to be with a lot of people warmly enjoying their food and wondering what the hell a TV crew was doing there. Actually, the apparent informality of Puglia belies some really impressive houses, particularly the old farms, the masserias, many of which have been turned into agriturismos, but my main reason for going to Puglia was to visit the house where Patience Gray had lived. She wrote an extraordinary book, *Honey From a Weed*, an account of living in various parts of the Mediterranean: the Greek island of Naxos, Carrara on the mainland of Italy, Catalonia, and the Salentine peninsula in Puglia. In the book she says: 'poverty rather than wealth gives the good things of life their true significance. Homemade bread rubbed with garlic and sprinkled with olive oil, shared with a flask of wine, between working people can be more convivial than any feast'. Her house was unadorned with any modern convenience. Her son Nick, who now lives there, said that she complained bitterly when he installed a refrigerator. She died in 2005. The locals all turned out for her funeral but I think her life and work would have been a bit of a mystery to them.

On the ferry from Brindisi to Corfu we were a little gloomy as our Land Rover had been stolen on our last night in Puglia and was, we assumed, travelling in the same sort of direction but to Albania on another ferry. (Amazingly, it was found in an olive grove a few weeks later.) We soon cheered up when we arrived in Corfu town. Arriving at dawn on any Greek island has a magical quality for me. The first time I arrived in Greece in the early 1970s was on that same ferry, seeing the cypress trees in the early morning light and gliding across the bay on the still water with the battlements and houses of the town itself in view. Corfu has got much busier since then. But like Mallorca, there are still lovely bits you can get away to. We travelled to the north of the island near Kassiopi, to a place called Perithia high up in the mountains, where snow settles in winter. The village had started emptying in the early 1960s when the locals realized they could leave their hard life and find jobs on the coast or in America and Australia. The population diminished until the village was abandoned but now, amazingly, it's being repopulated. There are three tavernas; many of the houses are still in ruins but some are already renovated. There's good food up there too, notably at Taverna Foros, run by Tomas and Vasso Siriotis, who served us an onion pie called kremithopita, and a dish called tsigarelli, of hot wild greens with tomato, cayenne pepper, olive oil and onion. But we liked the briam the most, a bit like ratatouille but much more vividly flavoured, with lots of dill (see my recipe on page 54). And if you go to Corfu, there's a really good fish restaurant at Boukari in the south. They have fresh calamari, great prawns and they do both of the local fish stews, bordetto and bianco, really well. We watched the owner, Spirios Karidis, prepare a plate of marinated anchovies while sitting under the tamarisk trees in the front of his restaurant. I haven't put the recipe in the book because fresh anchovies are hard to get, but it's easy. You fillet very fresh raw anchovies (or sardines, if you like), sprinkle them with salt and lemon juice, then serve them with a lick of olive oil, some parsley and a pinch of oregano.

And so to the final two countries on my trip: Turkey and Morocco. I confess a certain embarrassment at leaving out so many countries in the eastern Mediterranean and North Africa. To be honest, we spent too much time in Europe. I think, though, that Turkey right in the east and Morocco in the west cover a great deal of the cooking in between. We decided to go to eastern Turkey to be as non-European as possible, and so we found ourselves on the coast at Mersin near the Syrian boarder, with none of those dreamy beaches and little islands and fish restaurants of western Turkey. The coast is studded with oil refineries, steel mills and cheap holiday housing for the locals, but we really liked it. The food everywhere is full of character and the people are kind. We did find a few very attractive seaside places too, notably Narlikuyu and the surrounding area. There's a restaurant there called Lagos where they really know about their local fish. Lagos is the name of one of my favourite fish in the Mediterranean: the grouper. I watched one of the chefs there chopping a large grouper into perfectly even portions with a cleaver of considerable size, weight and sharpness. The steaks of fish were then taken with some reverence on a tray up some narrow steps in a tower next to the restaurant, to a little chamber where the chef of chefs operated the charcoal barbecue. The Turks' skill and reverence for barbecue cooking is unequalled anywhere else I've been. Not only was the grouper crisp on the outside and deliciously moist and firm inside, but at the same time the chef also cooked some small sweet onions and whole garlic bulbs. Experts in barbecue cooking over here or in America or Australia swear there is no fundamental difference in the taste of food cooked over charcoal or over gas – tell that to a Turk, I say! The Turks always use the same piece of equipment, which is called a *mangal*, one end of which is very hot, where the cooking is done; at the other end is a pile of charcoal heating up. They are constantly pulling partially heated charcoal down to the cooking end, so that you always get that wonderful perfume from the charcoal itself.

I was struck by the importance everyone puts into human skills: the baklava- and kebab-makers in Gaziantep, a little restaurant in Tarsus (where St Paul was born) specializing in the most exquisitely thin slices of liver cooked on charcoal, and again in Tarsus a perfect bowl of hummus where the emphasis was not just on the chickpea purée and the hot tahini but also the final presentation, where they drop a generous pinch of Aleppo pepper into fiercely hot oil and ladle it, sizzling, over the hummus.

The older I get as a chef, the more I realize the importance of getting things right. How to make the perfect chip or roast potato, where to buy the best tomatoes, the correct way of roasting beef or lamb, that sort of thing. A great deal of cooking in our country is about new ideas and pretty-looking food. It's a tremendous reassurance to go to somewhere like Turkey and see chefs doing things properly.

Finally, Morocco. I had first been there in my late twenties and loathed the place. It was dirty, the food was disgusting, the carpet salesmen drove us round the bend and worst of all it was Ramadan, that time in the Islamic calendar when no eating or drinking is allowed between sunrise and sunset, which can make even the most placid of human beings bad-tempered.

I don't know whether I've grown up a bit since the last time I went, or whether modern Morocco is a better place, or whether I've got more money now, or whether it's just that it wasn't Ramadan, or a little bit of all those, but everywhere I went was a delight. The fish stews and salads in Tangiers, the broad bean soup with olive oil and hot pepper in Chefchaouen or the beautiful tagines and couscous in Fes were just wonderful. I've related a number of my experiences in Morocco in the introduction to the recipes, but just a final memory: we were on our way from Tangier to Chefchaouen and stopped at a roadside café near Tetouan for coffees. It was a big place, three or four rooms at the back and a large seating area with an awning and a number of rather scruffy brown plastic tables and chairs. I suppose it was a bit off-putting, if you are used to motorway services, to notice that one of the counters at the back had cuts of lamb hanging from meat hooks. At one end was a charcoal hearth and a big pot sitting on a charcoal burner with another big pot on top of it and a film of plastic over the top. I wandered over to this and asked through our interpreter, Saad, what was going on. They were cooking lamb in steam. The charcoal was boiling water in the bottom pan and the steam was rising and cooking, very very gently, the lamb in the top, and the plastic film was to trap the flavours. There was nothing else, just very young lamb. We had to wait an hour, by which time the lamb was falling off the bone. They served up a big plate of it, because you eat communally with your fingers in Morocco, and with it a bowl of reduced tomato sauce with, I suspect, some chilli in it, a bowl of powdered cumin, some salt and some large muffin-shaped bread rolls which have semolina running through them, making them deliciously gritty. I sat down with Saad and Hicham, our driver. You take some lamb, sprinkle it with cumin and salt, break off a piece of bread, dip it in the tomato sauce, eat the lamb, eat the bread. I could just say it was so delicious it made me deliriously happy, but what I thought, more than that, was how grateful I was to Morocco for reminding me of the delight of simple things.

Fishing port, Tangier, Morocco

The souk, Tangier, Morocco, *opposite*: Fes, Morocco

MEZZE
KEMIA
MIA
TAPAS
ANTIPASTI

WHAT WE LOVE MOST ABOUT MEDITERRANEAN COOKING ARE
THOSE SMALL, INFORMAL DISHES THAT SEEM TO BE SERVED
EVERYWHERE IN GENEROUS QUANTITIES TO ACCOMPANY A
GLASS OF SOMETHING IN THE EARLY EVENING

Monastery of Vlacherna, Kanoi, Corfu

THIS RECIPE COMES FROM MENFI on the south coast of Sicily. I had met Nicolo and Ninny Ravidà's daughter, Natalia, in Palermo market and she introduced me to, amongst other unusual local vegetables, metre-long courgettes called tenerumi, plus a delightful pasta dish made from leaves (for which sadly you cannot get the ingredients outside Sicily). I discovered that her family made a peppery, green olive oil called Ravidà, and she invited me to her parents' place where they prepared a dinner with some of the best things Sicily has to offer, which included these sarde a beccafico. This seems to me to be the perfect recipe for sardines. Best eaten cold, ideally a day later, they are well worth the effort required (about one and a half hours' worth) to make them. *Makes 14–20*

SARDE A BECCAFICO: SARDINES STUFFED WITH PINE NUTS, CURRANTS, CAPERS, PARSLEY AND ORANGE ZEST

SICILY

14 large or 20 small sardines

1 orange, halved lengthways, then thinly sliced

About 20 fresh bay leaves

Salt and freshly ground black pepper

For the stuffing

50 g currants

4 tablespoons extra virgin olive oil, plus extra for drizzling

1 medium onion, finely chopped

4 garlic cloves, finely chopped

A pinch of crushed dried chillies

75 g fresh white breadcrumbs

2 tablespoons chopped flat-leaf parsley

15 g anchovy fillets in olive oil, drained and chopped

2 tablespoons small capers, chopped

Finely grated zest ½ small orange

1 tablespoon orange juice

25 g finely grated pecorino or parmesan cheese

50 g pine nuts, lightly toasted

To prepare the sardines, rub off the scales and rinse the fish under cold running water. Cut the head off each fish and discard. Then slit them open along the belly, down to the tail, and pull out the guts. Wash the cavities clean, then open up each fish in turn and place belly-side down on a chopping board. Press firmly along the backbone until the fish lies completely flat, then turn it over and pull away the backbone, snipping it off close to the tail. Remove any bones left behind with fish tweezers and then season lightly with salt.

Preheat the oven to 200°C/Gas Mark 6. For the stuffing, cover the currants in hot water and set them aside for 10 minutes to plump up. Heat the oil in a frying pan, add the onion, garlic and crushed dried chillies and cook gently for 6–7 minutes until the onion is soft but not browned. Take the pan off the heat and stir in the breadcrumbs, parsley, anchovies, capers, orange zest, orange juice, cheese and pine nuts. Drain the currants well and stir in, then season to taste with salt and pepper.

Spoon 1½–2 tablespoons of the stuffing (depending on the size of the fish) along the head

end of each sardine and roll them up towards the tail. Pack them tightly into an oiled shallow 20 x 30-cm baking dish, arranging them with their tails pointing upwards, and place a bay leaf and a half slice of orange between each one.

Season the fish lightly with salt and pepper, drizzle over a little more oil and bake for 20 minutes. Serve at room temperature or cold as part of an assortment of antipasti.

IN TURKEY, at least on the Mediterranean coast, I have two criteria for judging a good restaurant. One is the quality of the fried squid, and the second is the baba ghanoush, or moutabal as they often call it. The secret to a good baba ghanoush is achieving the right degree of smokiness by lightly charring the skin of the aubergine. Too much and it tastes as bad as the smoke from a hubbleybub; too little and it's bland and boring. But at its best it's a glorious dish. For me it will always bring back memories of a superb seafood restaurant in Istanbul called Balikçi Sabahattin in the Cankurtaran district, that elegantly tumble-down area around the Blue Mosque. Pomegranate seeds are optional, but if you can get them, do. *Serves 4–6*

BABA GHANOUSH:
SMOKY AUBERGINE PUREE WITH GARLIC, TAHINI AND LEMON JUICE
TURKEY

1 kg medium-sized aubergines

3 garlic cloves

3 tablespoons light tahini paste

1 teaspoon lemon juice

1 teaspoon extra virgin olive oil, plus extra
  to serve

The seeds from 1 pomegranate or coarsely
  chopped flat-leaf parsley, to garnish

Salt

Turkish flatbread or pitta bread, to serve

Pierce the aubergines near the stalk end with a fork to prevent them from bursting during cooking. Preheat the grill to its highest setting. Grill the aubergines for 40 minutes or so, depending on their size, turning them regularly until the skin is black, the insides feel very soft and they smell 'smoky'. This is what gives the dip its characteristic flavour.

Cut the aubergines in half lengthways and scoop out the soft creamy flesh into a bowl. Work it into a coarse paste with a potato masher.

Put the garlic cloves onto a chopping board, sprinkle with a large pinch of salt and crush into a smooth paste with the flat blade of a large knife. Add to the aubergines with the tahini, lemon juice, olive oil, and a little more salt to taste. Mix together well.

Transfer the baba ghanoush to a shallow serving bowl and spread it out, forming a slight hollow in the middle. Drizzle with some olive oil and then garnish with pomegranate seeds or chopped parsley. Serve with bread, for dipping.

SADLY, the reputations of tzatziki, guacamole and hummus have been tarnished by being offered in mass-produced form in every supermarket for consuming with those frightful taco chips for every drinks party from here to Wagawaga. A good tzatziki is a joy, but even in Greece there can be bad ones. The crux of a good one is to use an authentic Greek, full-fat ewe's milk yogurt. I don't think low-fat ones work. It also needs fresh dill or mint. I like to add a few spring onions, some freshly crushed garlic and a touch of vinegar to add bite. I also insist on eating it straight away while it's at its perfect best. *Serves 6*

TZATZIKI:
A CUCUMBER, GARLIC, DILL OR MINT AND GREEK YOGURT DIP
CORFU

1 large cucumber

2 garlic cloves

500 g natural Greek ewe's milk yogurt
  ('Total' is best)

75 g spring onions, trimmed and finely chopped

2 tablespoons chopped fresh dill or mint

2 tablespoons extra virgin olive oil

1 teaspoon white wine vinegar

Dill or mint sprigs or slices of cucumber, to
  garnish (optional)

Salt and freshly ground pepper

Lightly toasted pitta bread, to serve

Peel the skin of the cucumber away in strips – you want some but not all of it. Then coarsely grate the cucumber, pile it into the centre of a clean tea towel and squeeze out most of the excess liquid.

Put the garlic cloves onto a chopping board, sprinkle with a large pinch of salt and crush into a smooth paste with the flat blade of a large knife.

Tip the yogurt into a bowl and stir in the cucumber, garlic, spring onions, dill or mint, olive oil, vinegar and salt and pepper to taste. Serve garnished with dill or mint sprigs or a few peeled cucumber slices, if you like. Serve with pitta bread, for dipping.

THIS RECIPE COMES from Coleman Andrews's excellent book, *Catalan Cuisine*. Coleman Andrews is the editor of *Saveur* magazine, which I have found enormously influential since its appearance in 1994. With its authentic recipes and truthful photographs, no one has done more to draw attention to exciting, rugged local food from around the world. This is a typical example, uncompromising in flavour and glorious with a glass of ice-cold beer. The allioli is my addition. *Serves 6, as an appetizer*

BUNYOLS DE BACALLÁ
SALT COD FRITTERS WITH PARSLEY AND GARLIC
CATALONIA

500 g dried salt cod fillets
  (bacallá/bacalao)
1 fresh bay leaf
2 medium-sized floury potatoes (about
  200 g each), peeled and thinly sliced
Olive oil
50 g plain flour

3 medium eggs
2 garlic cloves, crushed
Leaves from 2 large sprigs flat-leaf parsley,
  chopped
Salt and freshly ground black pepper
Allioli (see page 211), to serve

Rinse any excess salt off the cod, then put into a large bowl and cover with cold water. Leave to soak in the fridge for 36–48 hours, changing the water 3–4 times a day. After this time, taste a small piece, and, if it still seems too salty, soak it for a bit longer. When you are happy with the degree of saltiness, drain and cut it into slightly smaller pieces.

Put the salt cod into a pan with the bay leaf and cover with fresh cold water. Bring to just below boiling point over a medium heat, then remove the pan from the heat and leave to stand for about 10 minutes.

Remove the salt cod from the water and leave to cool, setting the water to one side. When the fish has cooled, remove the skin and any bones and flake the flesh with a fork.

Put the potatoes into the pan of reserved salt cod cooking water, bring to the boil and cook for 10 minutes until tender. Drain well.

In another pan bring 300 ml water and 2 tablespoons olive oil to the boil, then remove from the heat and slowly beat in the flour to form a batter. Leave to cool slightly, then beat in the eggs, one at a time.

Mash the potatoes well in a large bowl and then mix in the salt cod, garlic and parsley. Add salt and pepper to taste. Then mix the salt cod mixture into the batter and cook over a low heat for about 10 minutes, stirring constantly, until the mixture thickens, has the consistency of mashed potatoes and will hold its shape when formed into balls. Leave to cool slightly and to thicken a little more.

Heat some oil for deep-frying to 190°C. Form the salt cod mixture into approximately 20 small balls using a spoon, and fry in batches, about 5–6 at a time, for 3 minutes or until a deep golden brown. Drain on kitchen paper and serve very hot, with allioli.

I COULD HAVE filled half the book with recipes for all the little dishes I tasted in the tapas bars in the Boqueria market in Barcelona. I remember giving a slightly shamefaced piece to camera about how the market was more of an attraction to me than the Gaudí architecture or the galleries full of Miró and Picasso. This is one of the dishes I tried there, where they had flavoured the mayonnaise with smoked pimentón. You can buy this relatively easily here now, and a pinch in a garlic and olive oil mayonnaise is a great accompaniment to really good squid. Dust the squid in a coarse flour to give a nice crisp texture. In Spain there is a flour specially milled for frying – harina de trigo; fine-ground semolina is the closest we can get to it here. *Serves 4 as a starter or 8 as part of a mixed mezze*

SQUID FRIED
IN OLIVE OIL WITH SMOKED PIMENTÓN AND GARLIC MAYONNAISE
CATALONIA

250 g cleaned squid
Harina de trigo or plain flour, for dusting
Olive oil, for shallow-frying
Salt and freshly ground black pepper
Lemon wedges, to serve

For the smoked pimentón and garlic mayonnaise
2 garlic cloves
200 g *Mayonnaise* (see page 211), made with olive oil and lemon juice
1 teaspoon smoked pimentón

For the smoked pimentón and garlic mayonnaise, put the garlic cloves onto a chopping board, sprinkle with a large pinch of salt and crush into a smooth paste with the flat blade of a large knife. Stir into the mayonnaise with the smoked pimentón and a little more salt to taste and set aside for a few minutes to allow the flavours time to develop.

Cut the squid pouches across into thin rings and separate the tentacles into pairs. Spread the rings and tentacles out onto a tray and season lightly with salt and pepper.

Pour olive oil in a large, deep frying pan to a depth of 1 cm and heat to 190°C over a medium-high heat. Toss the squid in the flour, knock off the excess and leave for 1–2 minutes so that the flour becomes slightly damp. This will give it a crisper finish.

Shallow-fry the squid in small batches for 1 minute until crisp and lightly golden. Drain briefly on kitchen paper, transfer to a warmed serving dish and repeat with the remaining squid. Serve hot with the smoked pimentón and garlic mayonnaise and lemon wedges.

ARANCINI MEANS 'little oranges', a reference to the colour, size and shape of these cheese- and ham-filled rice croquettes. The rice balls can be made in advance, then coated and deep-fried at the last minute. I had often made these, using recipes from Italian cook-books, but once in Sicily I discovered – particularly after consuming about half a dozen of them in the market at Catania – just how much cheese and ham they really should have, so this is a much beefed-up recipe; ideal to serve with drinks at a party. *Makes about 20*

ARANCINI DI RISO:
DEEP-FRIED BALLS OF RICE WITH HAM, PEAS, SAFFRON AND PROVOLONE CHEESE
SICILY

1–1.2 litres *Chicken stock*
  (see page 211)
A small pinch of saffron strands
45g unsalted butter
250 g risotto rice, such as arborio or
  carnaroli
1 egg yolk
25 g finely grated parmesan cheese
Salt and freshly ground black pepper

For the filling

75 g provolone piccante or mature
  gruyère cheese, cut into 5-mm dice
2 thin slices of prosciutto (air-dried ham,
  such as parma), cut into 1-cm squares
100 g cooked peas
2 eggs, beaten
150 g *Dried white breadcrumbs* **(see page**
  210)
Sunflower or vegetable oil, for deep-frying

First make a simple risotto. Bring the stock to the boil with the saffron, then leave over a low heat. Melt the butter in a medium-sized pan, add the rice and cook gently for about 2 minutes until the rice begins to look translucent. Add a ladleful of the hot stock and simmer, stirring constantly, until it has all been absorbed. Add another ladleful of stock and continue like this until the rice is tender and creamy but still a little *al dente* – this will take about 20–25 minutes. Stir in the egg yolk and parmesan and season to taste with salt and pepper. Spoon the risotto onto a shallow baking tray, press a sheet of clingfilm onto the surface and leave to go cold. Chill for 2 hours.

To form the arancini, dampen your hands with water and divide the risotto mixture into 30-g pieces. One piece at a time, flatten the mixture on the palm of one hand and put 2 cubes of cheese, a couple of pieces of prosciutto and 4 cooked peas into the centre, then shape the rice around the filling into a ball, patching up any gap with a little more of the risotto mixture.

Heat some oil for deep-frying to 180°C. Dip the rice balls into the beaten egg and then the breadcrumbs and deep-fry in batches for 3–4 minutes until they are crisp and golden brown. Drain on kitchen paper and serve immediately.

THESE ARE MORE COMMONLY KNOWN as kibbeh, the Lebanese name, but they are popular in Eastern Turkey too. The best ones, to me, have a slight heat from a little dried chilli and an aroma of cinnamon. The very best method, and you can do this with a little practice, is to work as thin a wall of the bulgar and lamb paste as possible, which leaves a good moist centre of spicy pine nut and lamb filling. If you don't want to make individual ones, then press half the coating mixture over the base of a shallow oiled baking tray, cover with the spiced lamb filling, then carefully cover with small, flattened pieces of the remaining coating mixture. Mark into a diamond pattern with a knife and bake at 180°C/Gas Mark 4 for 15–20 minutes until cooked through and lightly browned. *Makes about 40*

IÇLI KÖFTE: DEEP-FRIED MEATBALLS OF MINCED LAMB AND CRACKED WHEAT WITH PINE NUTS, GARLIC AND CINNAMON
TURKEY

Sunflower or vegetable oil for deep-frying

For the coating

225 g dried medium-grain bulgar wheat

450 g lean minced lamb, from the leg if possible

1 medium onion, chopped

1 teaspoon crushed dried chillies

4 tablespoons chopped flat-leaf parsley

Salt and freshly ground black pepper

For the filling

2 tablespoons olive oil

1 large onion, finely chopped

3 garlic cloves, crushed

15 g pine nuts

450 g lean minced lamb, from the leg if possible

¾ teaspoon salt

1 teaspoon lemon juice

For the spice mixture

2 whole green cardamom pods

4 cloves

1 teaspoon ground allspice

1 teaspoon crushed dried chillies

½ teaspoon ground cinnamon

2 teaspoons black peppercorns

Tzatziki (see page 23), to serve

Put the bulgar wheat into a bowl and cover with plenty of boiling water. Leave to soak for 10 minutes, or until just tender but still *al dente*. You still want it to have a little bite to it. Tip into a sieve and leave to drain well, then tip it into the centre of a clean tea towel and squeeze out any excess moisture.

For the outer layer of the meatballs, put the minced lamb, onion, crushed dried chillies, chopped parsley, 1½ teaspoons of salt and some pepper into a food processor and blend together for 1 minute. Remove two-thirds of the meat mixture and add one-third of the soaked bulgar wheat to the mixture still in the food processor. Blend together for about 1 minute until it forms a soft, smooth paste, then transfer it to a bowl and repeat twice more with another third of the minced lamb and bulgar wheat.

To make the spice mixture, grind everything together into a fine powder. I have an electric coffee grinder for doing this. This will make more than you need but it will store well in a screw-top jar.

For the filling, heat the olive oil in a saucepan over a medium heat. Add the onion and garlic and cook until the onion is soft and lightly browned – about 10 minutes. Add the pine nuts and fry until they are lightly golden, then add 1 tablespoon of the spice mixture and fry for a further minute. Add the minced lamb and fry for 4–5 minutes until all the meat is cooked. Stir in the salt and lemon juice and leave to cool.

With slightly wet hands, take a 25-g piece of the lamb and bulgar-wheat mixture and roll it into a ball. Make a hole in the centre of it with your finger and gradually shape the mixture into a thin walled 'pot' in the palm of your hand. Spoon 1 heaped teaspoon of the filling into the hole, then pinch the top of the 'pot' together to seal it. They traditionally have a point so they look a bit like a spinning top, but don't worry if you can't manage this.

Heat some oil for deep-frying to 190°C. Deep-fry the meatballs a few at a time for 2–3 minutes until golden brown. Drain on kitchen paper and serve hot with tzatziki.

IT IS HARD TO THINK OF A DISH that better exemplifies the expression 'less is more' than bruschetta. It's all about the great wood-fired sourdough bread of places in Italy like Puglia, and the best extra virgin olive oil. Warm grilled bread with the flavour of the fire served with some olive oil, black pepper, sea salt and tomato appears all over the Mediterranean. When in Cornwall I might also crave some, maybe with a little torn basil or wild rocket, or even a sliver of salted anchovy or a fold of wafer-thin prosciutto on top. But there's also another very special topping for bruschetta: puréed broad beans, a vivid bright green with the warm flavour of pulse, garlic, olive oil and mint. *Serves 4*

BRUSCHETTE:
TWO BRUSCHETTAS: TOMATO AND BASIL, AND BROAD BEAN AND MINT
PUGLIA

4 x 1-cm thick slices of country-style bread

1 garlic clove, peeled

Best extra virgin olive oil

Sea salt and freshly ground black pepper

For the tomato topping

1 large, ripe beef tomato, skinned

A couple of basil leaves, torn

For the broad bean topping

250 g shelled broad beans, ideally fresh but frozen will do

1 small garlic clove

1 teaspoon lemon juice

2½ tablespoons extra virgin olive oil

2–3 mint leaves, finely shredded

Somehow you need the taste of flame in the bread, so either grill the bread over a barbecue or else toast it and then, holding the slice with a pair of tongs, slightly singe one side over a naked gas flame. On a toasting fork in front of an open fire would also be perfect. Rub the singed side of the toast with a peeled clove of garlic. Drizzle with extra virgin olive oil and sprinkle with a little sea salt and freshly ground black pepper.

For the tomato topping, cut the tomato into 1-cm-thick slices and then roughly cut into small chunky pieces. Spoon some onto each slice of prepared bread, scatter over a little basil and sprinkle with a little more oil, sea salt and pepper.

For the broad bean topping, drop the beans and the garlic clove into a pan of boiling salted water, bring back to the boil and simmer for 5 minutes or until they are tender. Drain, reserving a little of the cooking liquid, refresh under cold water and leave to cool. Slip the beans out of their skins and put them into a food processor with the cooked piece of garlic and lemon juice. Whizz to a purée, slowly adding the olive oil. If the mixture is very thick, add a little of the reserved cooking liquid – the purée should have the consistency of thick hummus. Season to taste with salt and roughly spread onto the prepared bread. Drizzle with a little more oil and scatter over a little mint.

TO EXPLAIN HOW the Pugliese love their vegetables, it is best to relate an evening we spent at a restaurant in Ostuni, called Don Chischiote. In addition to the normal antipasti, they presented a big bowl of peas in the pod. They were clearly fresh off the vine. We devoured them with the fresh bread and olive oil, remarking how odd people back home would think it if you sent out fresh peas but vowing to do it when back in Padstow. The next day, driving to the coast for a lunch of sea urchin roes with pasta, we passed six or seven carts laden with fresh peas and broad beans. We bought about five kilos of them. I was still enjoying them when we got to Corfu. This common Italian dish is never better than with those sweet, fresh green peas from Puglia. *Serves 4 as a tapas or side dish*

PEAS WITH ONIONS, PARMA HAM AND OLIVE OIL
PUGLIA

100 ml extra virgin olive oil
12 button onions or small shallots, peeled
1 x 100 g thick slice of parma ham,
    or ham trimmings or pancetta
2 garlic cloves, thinly sliced
450 g freshly shelled or frozen peas
2 tablespoons roughly chopped flat-leaf
    parsley
Salt and freshly ground black pepper

Heat 2 tablespoons of the olive oil in a medium-sized pan, add the onions and fry until lightly golden on all sides. Add 2 tablespoons water, cover and simmer for 5 minutes until just tender.

Meanwhile, chop the parma ham, trimmings or the pancetta into small pieces. Uncover the pan, add the remaining oil, garlic and ham or pancetta and cook for a minute or two. Add the peas, ¾ teaspoon salt and plenty of black pepper.

Cover and simmer gently for 15 minutes until the peas are very tender and the flavours have had time to amalgamate. Stir in the parsley 2 minutes before the end.

IN MOROCCO salads can be made from raw vegetables or can be cooked dishes designed to be served at room temperature together with little bowls of olives and toasted almonds. All go together to make kemia (similar to eastern Mediterranean mezze). If you are lucky enough to be staying in a good riad – a traditional Moroccan house built round a shady courtyard – in somewhere like Fes, you'll often find them serving a first course consisting of eight or ten of these warm and raw vegetable salads, with loads of fresh flatbread. The recurring problem for me is finding a corner in which to fit the rest of the meal, having swooped on such an abundance of delicious first-course dishes. Of the cooked vegetable dishes, one of the most delicious is chakchouka. *Serves 4–6 as part of a selection*

CHAKCHOUKA:
GRILLED GREEN PEPPER AND TOMATO SALAD WITH PAPRIKA AND CUMIN
MOROCCO

3 large green peppers

50 ml sunflower oil

25 ml olive oil, plus a little extra to serve

3 garlic cloves, crushed

1 teaspoon sweet paprika

A large pinch of cayenne pepper

1½ teaspoons ground cumin

450 g vine-ripened tomatoes, coarsely grated and the skins discarded

1 small bunch fresh coriander, coarsely chopped

Salt

Crusty fresh bread, to serve

Grill the green peppers over a naked gas flame or under a hot grill until the skins have blackened and the flesh is soft: about 20–25 minutes. Rub off the blackened skins under cold running water and then coarsely chop the flesh, discarding the stalk and seeds.

Put the sunflower and olive oils and the garlic into a frying pan and, as soon as the garlic starts to sizzle, add the paprika, cayenne pepper, cumin and tomatoes. Leave to simmer until reduced to a thickish sauce in which the oil is showing signs of starting to split from the tomatoes.

Stir in the roasted green peppers and some salt to taste and leave to simmer for 3–4 minutes more. Stir in the chopped coriander and drizzle with a little more olive oil. Spoon into one large or a few slightly smaller shallow dishes and serve at room temperature with plenty of crusty fresh bread.

AT THE END of the river Ebro in Catalonia is a little fishing port called Sant Carles de la Ràpita. It's a tourist destination in the summer, with the important characteristic that it's for the locals. We spent a few days filming there during a week of bull running. The running in Sant Carles is done in a makeshift arena of scaffolding and parked trucks. There are two or three iron cages in the arena, and steep wooden ramps up which the bulls are persuaded to charge. Most of the male population of the town, or so it seemed to me, run around irritating the bulls and then skip behind a barrier or slip through the bars of a cage when chased. Occasionally the bulls catch someone. I saw one man trampled underfoot and, if not gored, buffeted by the horns so that he was bleeding profusely. I joined a group on the platform at the top of one of the cages, drinking beer and eating Iberico ham sliced from the leg. It's scary running across the arena to the cage: timing is everything. It made the ham and beer taste that much better. The bulls are young and enthusiastically angry but after a while they tire so a cow is released into the ring, who rounds them up as if to say: 'Come on, boys, time to go home.' This mussel dish is the sort of food that was being sold outside the arena in the many little booths. *Serves 6*

GRILLED STUFFED MUSSELS
WITH GARLIC, PARSLEY AND ANCHOVY BREADCRUMBS
CATALONIA

1.5 kg mussels, cleaned

50 ml dry white wine

3 tablespoons olive oil

1 small onion, finely chopped

2 garlic cloves, finely chopped

1 x 50-g tin anchovy fillets in olive oil

25 g capers, rinsed and chopped

2 tablespoons chopped flat-leaf parsley

A good pinch of peperoncino or crushed dried chillies

75 g fresh white breadcrumbs

Salt and freshly ground black pepper

Preheat the grill to high. Heat a large pan over a high heat. Add the mussels and wine, cover with a lid and cook over a high heat, shaking the pan now and then, for about 2 minutes, until all the mussels have opened (discarding any that do not). Tip them into a colander to drain and when cool enough to handle, remove half of the shell, leaving the mussels in the other shell. For ease of eating, release the mussels from the inside of each shell, and put the shells side by side on a large baking tray or in 6 individual shallow ovenproof dishes.

Heat the olive oil in medium-sized frying pan, add the onion and garlic and cook gently until soft and lightly golden. Reduce the heat slightly, add the anchovies and their oil and cook a little longer until they have melted into the onions. Add the capers, parsley, peperoncino or crushed chillies and cook for 1 more minute. Then take off the heat and stir in the breadcrumbs and some seasoning to taste.

Spoon some of the breadcrumb mixture on top of each mussel and grill for 4 minutes or until crisp and golden. Serve immediately.

ONE OF THE HIGHLIGHTS of my visit to Mino and Carol Maggi's *trullo* at Locorotondo was the superb focaccia they made and generously handed out to everybody that morning. For those not in the know, the *trulli* are the little beehive-shaped houses, the most distinctive feature of this area, particularly in Locorotondo, and Alberobello just down the road. You'd swear that JRR Tolkien visited here some years ago and hit on the idea of the hobbit houses in the Shire, so small, cosy and traditional are they. My friend Anna Maggio, who accompanied us on our Italian journeys as translator, organizer and expert on all matters culinary, has bought one just outside Ostuni and renovated it into an amazingly atmospheric house set in an olive grove. She attested to the quality of the focaccia, the recipe for which follows. *Makes 1 bread of 30 x 40 cm*

FOCACCIA
WITH ROSEMARY AND ROCK SALT
PUGLIA

600 g strong plain flour

1½ teaspoons salt

2 teaspoons easy-blend yeast

Leaves from four 20-cm rosemary sprigs

360 ml warm water

2 tablespoons olive oil, plus extra for drizzling

1 teaspoon coarse rock salt

Sift the flour, salt and yeast into a large mixing bowl and stir in half of the rosemary leaves. Make a well in the centre and add almost all the water and the olive oil. Gradually mix the flour into the liquid, adding some or all the remaining water if necessary to give a soft dough. Turn the dough out onto a lightly floured surface and knead for 10 minutes until smooth and elastic.

Place the dough into a cleaned, lightly oiled bowl, cover with clingfilm and leave somewhere warm for 1–1½ hours until doubled in size.

Cut out a piece of non-stick baking paper to fit the base of a 30 x 40 cm shallow baking tray that is about 2.5 cm deep – a Swiss roll tin would be ideal. Put the baking paper on the work surface. Knock the excess air out of the dough, tip it out of the bowl onto the baking paper and press it out into an even layer. Lift the dough on the paper into the tin, cover loosely with clingfilm and place in warm place for another 1 hour or until doubled in size.

Preheat the oven to 240°C/Gas Mark 9, or as high as your oven will go. Uncover the dough and drizzle with a little more olive oil. Scatter with the remaining rosemary leaves and the rock salt, and then push your fingertips into the surface of the dough to form dimples.

Bake for 15–18 minutes until golden brown. Remove and leave to cool on a wire rack. To serve, cut the bread into squares or small chunky slices.

I HAVE BEEN SLOW-COOKING octopus and cuttlefish in olive oil with aromatic herbs and spices for some time, and this was inspired by the spicing of a lot of dishes in the Mediterranean, especially Corfu. The drawback with boiling octopus, as is the norm in Greece and Italy, is you don't get any of those precious juices you get from slow-cooking. I've amalgamated them into a dressing here with some olive oil and lemon juice. *Serves 4 as a starter or 8 as part of a mixed mezze*

SPICED OCTOPUS SALAD
WITH PARSLEY
CORFU

1 octopus, weighing about 0.75–1 kg

50 ml extra virgin olive oil

7.5-cm piece cinnamon stick

4 cloves

6 allspice berries

1 teaspoon black peppercorns

1 teaspoon sea salt flakes

To finish

¾ teaspoon lemon juice

1 tablespoon coarsely chopped flat-leaf parsley

2 teaspoons extra virgin olive oil

Preheat the oven to 110°C/Gas Mark ¼. To clean the octopus, turn the body pouch inside out and pull away the entrails and bone-like strips sticking to the sides. Locate the stomach sac, which is about the size of an avocado stone, and cut it away. Wash the octopus well inside and out and then turn the body right-side out again. Press the beak and the soft surround out from the centre of the tentacles, cut out and discard.

Put the octopus into a small casserole with the olive oil, cinnamon, cloves, allspice berries, peppercorns and salt. Cover with a well-fitting lid and bake for 2 hours or until tender.

Remove the casserole from the oven and lift the octopus onto a plate. Strain the cooking juices into a small pan and boil rapidly until reduced by about half and really well flavoured. Leave to cool along with the octopus.

When the octopus is cool, cut off the tentacles and slice each one across on the diagonal into slices about 5 mm thick. Cut the body into similar-sized pieces.

Put the octopus into a bowl and stir in 3 tablespoons of the reduced cooking liquor, the lemon juice and parsley. Toss together well, spoon into a shallow serving dish and drizzle with the extra virgin olive oil just before serving at room temperature.

OTHER MEZZE DISHES:

Tabbouleh (page 42)

Caponata (page 59)

Carrot salad with orange flower water and mint (page 66)

Beetroot salad with cinnamon and preserved lemon (page 67)

Grilled prawns with ouzo, tomatoes, chilli and feta (page 87)

Gigandes plaki (page 176)

Chickpea, chorizo, tomato and spinach stew (page 170)

Skate with tomato, saffron and garlic (page 99)

HERBS WEEDS
SALAD LEAVES
AND OTHER GREENS

PERHAPS THE MAIN REASON FOR
THE HEALTHINESS OF THE MEDITERRANEAN
DIET IS THE ASTONISHING VARIETY OF
GREEN LEAVES THAT FIND THEMSELVES IN
SALADS, STEWS AND PIES

Alcudia, Mallorca

I HAVE A LIFE-LONG enthusiasm for watching people making produce by hand, swiftly and deftly as if it was the simplest thing in the world. Peeling shrimps, picking crabs, filleting tuna, throwing sheets of filo pastry across a table. I absolutely know I can do it just as easily, which is not quite how it turns out. So it is with orecchiette, the round, fingertip-shaped pasta from Puglia, whose name means 'little ears'. For five minutes I watched it being made and it seemed so easy. You roll the pasta dough into a long rope, cut a tiny slice off the end, then pull it away at the same time as pushing your finger into the centre, to make a perfect little ear every time. It doesn't always work, but this dish certainly does: pasta with garlic, olive oil, anchovy, a dash of chilli and some cavalo nero, purple sprouting broccoli or the traditional turnip tops (*cime de rape*). The object is to cook the greens with the pasta, then drain both and toss with the oil and anchovy mixture. In Italy they put a dash of the cooking water in with the pasta and toss everything together vigorously. The result is a pleasingly emulsified sauce. *Serves 4*

ORECCHIETTE
WITH CAVALO NERO
PUGLIA

500 g dried orecchiette pasta

500 g cavalo nero, turnip tops or young
   purple sprouting broccoli

6 tablespoons extra virgin olive oil

3 garlic cloves, thinly sliced

½ teaspoon crushed dried chillies

6 anchovy fillets in olive oil

Freshly grated pecorino or parmesan
   cheese, to serve (optional)

Salt and freshly ground black pepper

Bring 4.5 litres water to the boil in a large saucepan with 8 teaspoons salt. Meanwhile, trim any large stalks from the cavalo nero and cut any large leaves into approximately 10-cm pieces.

Add the pasta to the boiling water and cook for 12 minutes. Four minutes before the pasta is cooked, add the cavalo nero to the pan and cook for the remaining time, until the greens are tender and the pasta is *al dente*.

Meanwhile, put the olive oil, garlic and chilli flakes into a large deep frying pan and place over a medium heat. As soon as the garlic begins to sizzle, leave it to cook for a few seconds and then add the anchovy fillets and break them up with a wooden spoon until they have 'melted' into the oil. Remove from the heat.

Drain the pasta and cavalo nero and just before all the water has drained off them, add them to the frying pan and toss together well. Place over a high heat and shake around for a few seconds until the cooking liquid still clinging to the pasta and leaves has amalgamated with the oil and the cooked leaves to create a sauce. Divide between warmed bowls and serve sprinkled with some pecorino or parmesan cheese if you wish.

WHY IS IT THAT some dishes get murdered by well-meaning enthusiasts who have no idea what the original tastes like? Here's a list and you'll know what I mean: quiche, Greek salad, bean or cold pasta combinations and, above all, tabbouleh, which is so often wet, mushy and tasteless. So what do I think is the secret of a good tabbouleh? Only wash the bulgar, don't soak it, and leave it to soften slightly in just the juices from the tomatoes. Don't overdo the amount of bulgar, and use plenty of fresh, flat-leaf parsley, a judicious amount of spring onions, a touch of mint and lemon, and some good extra virgin olive oil. *Serves 4*

TABBOULEH:
PARSLEY, MINT, BULGAR WHEAT AND TOMATO SALAD
TURKEY

100 g fine-grain bulgar wheat

200 g (about 2) firm, vine-ripened tomatoes,
   finely diced

80-g bunch of flat-leaf parsley

A small bunch of mint

3 spring onions, trimmed and thinly sliced

1 tablespoon lemon juice

3 tablespoons extra virgin olive oil

The smaller leaves from the centre of 2
   romaine or cos lettuce hearts

Salt

Put the bulgar wheat in a sieve and rinse briefly under cold water. Drain well, then tip onto a clean tea towel and press out the excess water. Tip into a bowl and stir in the chopped tomatoes. The juices from them will be sufficient to soften the wheat. Set aside for 45 minutes.

Wash the bunch of parsley well in cold water, shake off the excess and dry really well. Then, holding the bunch tightly in one hand, slice the leaves across as finely as you can with a very sharp knife until you have about 60 g, but don't chop them. Discard the stalks (or save them for another dish or for making stock). Slice the mint leaves across in the same way to yield 1 tablespoon.

Stir the parsley and mint into the bulgar wheat with the spring onions, lemon juice, olive oil and some salt to taste. Spoon the salad onto a large shallow serving plate and either tuck the lettuce leaves in round the edge or stick them in a bowl and serve them separately. Serve straight away.

THERE ARE MANY pleasant surprises to be had eating out in Turkey, none more so than the abundance of salads. This recipe comes from a fish restaurant called Lagos in the fishing village of Narlikuyu, near Mersin in eastern Turkey. In addition to this, they served a salad of young spinach leaves, some hard, tangy goat's cheese, raw onions and chillies, small onions cooked on charcoal, pickled chillies with pickled carrots, green beans and rock samphire, some whole chargrilled bulbs of new-season garlic, a big bowl of local olives with slices of lemon, and some freshly baked *pide* bread. Lastly, and most importantly, were the thick steaks of grouper (*lagos*) cooked by the master chef over lumpy charcoal in a tiny barbecue room at the top of a steep flight of stairs. Often the salads are dressed with oil and lemon juice and thick, sticky pomegranate molasses, which is almost like balsamic vinegar. *Serves 6*

TURKISH
MIXED LEAF SALAD
TURKEY

1 large romaine or cos lettuce,
   outer leaves removed and
   discarded

100 g red cabbage, core removed,
   finely shredded

1 medium carrot, peeled and
   coarsely grated

1 ripe tomato, halved, seeded
   and cut into small pieces

15 g wild rocket

15 g flat-leaf parsley leaves

For the dressing

½ small garlic clove

½ teaspoon salt

50 ml extra virgin olive oil

2 tablespoons lemon juice

½ teaspoon caster sugar

Freshly ground black pepper

Cut the romaine or cos lettuce across into 1-cm wide strips. Wash and dry well and mix in a bowl with all the other ingredients.

For the dressing, crush the garlic into a paste on a board with the salt, using the flat blade of a knife, and put into a small bowl with the olive oil, lemon juice, sugar and a little black pepper. Toss through the salad just before serving.

THESE REMIND ME of a holiday in Crete I had many years ago. It was in a village just outside Chania where for the first time, after many trips all over Greece, I finally found a restaurant where the cooking was excellent. Greek cooking was a bit of a joke to us back then, but this was something amazing. There were snails in a sauce made with local wine vinegar, beautiful kleftiko served because it was Easter, stamnagathi, or boiled wild chicory, with olive oil and lemon, and the most sublime spanakopita. The restaurant was run by a young couple, and the wife was the cook. I was in love with her by the time we left. It was not so much to do with her looks, which were very nice, but her sublime cooking. My enduring memories are of these feta and spinach pies, snow on the mountains, wild fennel in the meadows and that curious slightly eerie call of scops owls at dusk. *Makes about 18–20*

SPANAKOPITA:
SPINACH, MINT AND FETA PASTRIES
CORFU

500 g spinach

1 tablespoon olive oil

½ small onion, finely chopped

2 spring onions, trimmed and
  finely chopped

100 g Greek feta cheese

1 large egg

1 tablespoon finely grated Greek kefalotiri
  cheese or parmesan cheese

A pinch of freshly grated nutmeg

2 tablespoons chopped fresh mint

250–275-g packet filo pastry (about 6 sheets)

100 g butter, melted

Salt and freshly ground black pepper

Wash the spinach, remove the large stalks and dry. Finely shred the leaves. Heat the olive oil in a large pan, add the onion and cook gently until soft but not browned. Add the spinach a handful at a time, until it has all wilted down. Tip into a colander and drain, press out all the excess liquid, then return to the pan with the spring onions and cook for 1 minute. Leave to cool.

Crumble the feta cheese into a mixing bowl and mash with a fork to remove any really large lumps but leave it a little chunky. Mix in the eggs, grated kefalotiri or parmesan, the spinach mixture, nutmeg, mint and salt and pepper to taste.

Preheat the oven to 180°C/Gas Mark 4. Unroll the sheets of filo pastry and cut the stack lengthways into strips about 7.5 cm wide. Brush the top layer with melted butter. Place a heaped teaspoonful of the filling in the centre of one strip, at the end nearest to you, and fold one bottom corner of the pastry diagonally over the filling, so that the corner touches the opposite side to make a triangle. Then fold over the filled triangular corner, and continue folding it along the whole strip into a triangular parcel. Repeat to make all the spanakopita.

Brush the undersides of each one with more butter and place on a lightly buttered baking tray. Brush the tops with butter and bake for 25 minutes until crisp and richly golden brown. Serve hot while the pastry is still crisp and brittle; it will soften the longer they are left to stand.

THERE ARE LOTS OF THESE slow-simmered vegetable stews all over the Mediterranean. I particularly like this one, which seems to be a celebration of all the best vegetables on the island, with plenty of deep-green olive oil. In no other dish will the quality of the vegetables be more important. It's simply not worth making this at any time other than late summer and early autumn, when everything is bursting with mellow fruitfulness. Apparently, *sympetherio* means 'fellow in-laws', the idea being that all these different vegetables must learn to get on in the pot as they work together to build a harmonious marriage of flavours. For the wild greens, known in Greek as *horta*, use a mixture of any of the following leaves: red Swiss chard, spinach, rocket, watercress, dandelions, sorrel, wild chicory, beet greens. *Serves 4*

SYMPETHERIO:
A SLOW-COOKED STEW OF GREEN BEANS, OKRA, AUBERGINES AND WILD GREENS
CORFU

120 ml extra virgin olive oil

1 large onion, chopped

2 fat garlic cloves, crushed

250 g dwarf green beans, trimmed

250 g small waxy potatoes, such as Charlotte, peeled and quartered or cut into chunks if large

4 globe artichokes

250 g okra, trimmed (optional)

250 g aubergines, topped and tailed and cut into 5-cm chunks

1 x 400-g can chopped tomatoes

250 g courgettes, trimmed and cut into 5-cm chunks

75 g mixed wild greens (see above)

Salt and freshly ground black pepper

Crusty fresh bread, to serve

Heat the olive oil in a large flameproof casserole. Add the onion and cook over a medium heat for 7–8 minutes until soft but not brown. Add the garlic and cook for a further 1–2 minutes.

Add the green beans, potatoes and ½ teaspoon salt and stir together well. Pour in some water to just cover the vegetables – about 450 ml – cover and simmer for 15 minutes.

Meanwhile, prepare the artichokes. Cut off the top half and the stalk, then slice away the dark green outer leaves, exposing the lighter green and tender part.

Uncover the stew, add the okra if using, aubergines, artichoke hearts and tomatoes and stir together well. Adjust the seasoning with salt and pepper and leave to simmer, uncovered, for 20 minutes. Then add the courgettes, and simmer for a further 20 minutes until all the vegetables are tender and the liquid has reduced. Stir in the wild greens and cook for a further 2 minutes until they have wilted down into the sauce. Serve warm or at room temperature with plenty of crusty fresh bread.

THIS PURÉE OF DRIED broad beans topped with boiled wild chicory is probably one of the most popular vegetable-based dishes in Puglia. As I've enthused elsewhere in this book, dried broad beans have been a bit of a revelation to me. Watching Maria Lisi make this in her ancient but robust restaurant kitchen at La Spagnula just outside Ostuni, I marvelled at the simplicity of country cooking in Italy and how it always seems to exactly hit the spot. My purée is accompanied by cavalo nero instead of the more traditional wild chicory because it's so difficult to get bitter greens in the UK – things like treviso, cultivated dandelions and, of course, wild chicory itself – though they are bound to arrive in our supermarkets and vegetable shops before too long, as they have already done in Australia. Curly kale and even sprouting broccoli is also exquisite with this. *Serves 4*

FAVE E CICORIA:
BROAD BEAN PURÉE WITH BITTER GREENS
PUGLIA

450 g dried skinned and split broad beans (fave
  sgusciate, see page 212 for suppliers)
6 tablespoons extra virgin olive oil, plus extra
  to serve
250 g young cavalo nero, washed well and any
  tough stalks removed
2 pinches of crushed dried chillies
1 small garlic clove, finely chopped
Salt

Wash the beans well and then put them into a bowl and cover with plenty of cold water. Leave them to soak overnight.

The following day, drain the beans and rinse in cold water. Put them into a saucepan and cover with 1 litre of water. Bring to the boil and leave to simmer, uncovered, for 1 hour until the water has evaporated and the cooked beans are soft enough to be mashed.

Remove the pan from the heat, add 1 teaspoon of salt, cover and set aside for 15 minutes. Then mash them into a coarse purée, whisk in 4 tablespoons of the olive oil, cover and set aside to keep warm.

Bring a large pan of well-salted water to the boil. Drop in the cavalo nero and cook for 3 minutes until just tender. Drain well.

Warm another 2 tablespoons of olive oil in a sauté pan or large frying pan with the crushed dried chillies and garlic. As soon as it starts to sizzle, add the cavalo nero and toss together gently. Season with salt and pepper.

Reheat the broad bean purée if necessary and spoon on to warm plates. Pile the cavalo nero on top, drizzle with a little more olive oil and serve.

THE GREEKS CALL the greens and herbs they gather from the hills and mountains, especially in spring, by the general name of *horta*. In the market in Corfu town I met a lady called Effie who was selling wild greens. She had spent twenty years as a hairdresser in Melbourne and appeared to have come home mainly because she couldn't gather her beloved wild chicories, thistles, peas, poppies and sow's thistle in Australia. We went picking on a sunny spring morning in a meadow splashed with the reds, yellows and blues of wild flowers, against a background of cypress trees and mountains. I was back in Cornwall a month later when our wild greens were about as advanced. Walking through the meadows beyond the church at Morwenstow, with a beautiful view of the bay beyond, I noticed lots of the plants in the hedgerow but I had no one like Effie to give me guidance as to what was good to eat. Bitter is a flavour we don't understand much, though any member of the chicory family is naturally bitter and easy to grow. By using some ruggedly flavoured brassicas like curly kale, cavalo nero, watercress or rocket, together with members of the beet family such as chard, and some spinach or sorrel, you will get something close to the real thing. Slipping in the odd dandelion leaf and some wild garlic is also a good idea. Serve the chunky omelette with a simple tomato and onion salad and some bread. *Serves 6*

North-eastern Corfu

BAKED GREEK OMELETTE
WITH WILD GREENS, HERBS, LEEKS AND FETA
CORFU

3 tablespoons extra virgin olive oil

250 g leeks, trimmed, cleaned and thinly sliced

250 g mixed leaves (see above), washed, dried and shredded

8 large eggs, lightly beaten

3 tablespoons chopped mint

3 tablespoons chopped dill

175 g Greek feta cheese, crumbled

25 g grated Greek kefalotiri cheese or parmesan cheese

Salt and freshly ground black pepper

Preheat the oven to 160°C/Gas Mark 3. Heat 2 tablespoons of the olive oil in a deep frying pan over a medium heat. Add the leeks and cook gently for 10 minutes until soft.

Add the remaining oil and the mixed leaves to the pan and cook for 3–4 minutes until they have wilted down and are just tender.

Tip the greens into a bowl and add the eggs, mint, dill, crumbled feta, grated kefalotiri or parmesan cheese, ½ teaspoon salt and some black pepper. Oil a shallow, round, 20-cm non-stick cake tin, pour in the mixture and bake for about 45 minutes or until just set.

THIS SAUCE FROM CORSICA is designed to use the abundance of wild herbs from the island, but I've had to modify it a little because you can't get the same herbs here in Britain. Like the Italian salsa verde, this is a simple, easy-to-make sauce for any grilled fish or meat, and I think it is perfection with a grilled veal chop. I've suggested two ways of cooking veal chops – under the grill or on the barbecue. Carefully cooked on the barbecue they are superb. I keep a box of oak chips under my barbecue and scatter a few through the bars to give a faint flavour of wood smoke. With a thick cut of meat like this, I would always use all three burners on my barbecue for searing the meat, but then turn the middle one off and continue to cook by indirect heat so there is no danger of a flare-up, which if not checked will scorch and blacken the meat. If you are in the market for a barbecue, I recommend getting one with a lid. It makes it easier to cook more carefully, and in all weathers – I've always been a fan of cooking outdoors in mid-December. *Serves 4*

GRILLED VEAL CHOPS
WITH A SAUCE OF WATERCRESS, CAPERS, SORREL AND TARRAGON
CORSICA

4 x veal chops, cut about 2.5 cm thick
  and each weighing about 500 g
For the green sauce
2 garlic cloves
4 tablespoons capers, well rinsed
20 g flat-leaf parsley leaves

10 g mint leaves
30 g mixed watercress and tarragon
6 tablespoons extra virgin olive oil, plus
  extra for brushing
Juice ½ lemon (about 1½ tablespoons)
Salt and freshly ground black pepper

If you are using a charcoal barbecue, light it 40 minutes before you want to start cooking. If you are using a gas barbecue, light it 10 minutes beforehand. Otherwise preheat the grill to high.

For the sauce, coarsely chop the garlic cloves and then put into a small food processor with the capers, parsley, mint, mixed leaves and oil and blend for a few seconds into a coarse paste. Spoon into a bowl and stir in the lemon juice, ½ teaspoon salt and 20 turns of the black pepper mill.

Brush the veal chops on either side with a little more oil and season well with salt and pepper. Cook for 6–8 minutes on each side until cooked through but still moist inside and with a slight pink blush. If you have a meat thermometer it should register 60°C in the centre of the meat. Serve with the sauce.

ARTICHOKES AUBERGINES

AND THE MEDITERRANEAN GARDEN

BEAUTIFUL VEGETABLES SWEETENED
BY THE SUN: THIS IS THE GLORY
OF THE MEDITERRANEAN DIET

Soller, northern Mallorca

BRIAM: TAVERNA FOROS'S OVEN-BAKED SUMMER VEGETABLES WITH DILL

CORFU

I LIKE BUTTERFLYING a small leg of lamb and carefully cooking it on a barbecue, and this would be the perfect accompaniment. It seems to me that the Greeks excel at vegetable dishes like this (have a look at my recipe for sympetherio on page 46). Watching Vasso, Tomas Siriotis's wife, make this dish at their restaurant, Foros, in the village of Perithia way up in the mountains of Corfu, I was struck by the robustness with which she seasoned it: plenty of salt and lots of black pepper in each layer, a veritable bush of dill and no sparing of the olive oil either. I noticed this everywhere in Greece, forceful and passionate cooking, like the nature of the people themselves. Dishes like this are so simple and yet so good. You may wonder why this recipe is for such a large quantity and the answer is the Greeks just don't do small. There are always lots of vegetables to hand, and it's just as good served cold the next day. *Serves 8*

150 ml extra virgin olive oil, plus extra for oiling the tin

500 g waxy main crop potatoes, such as Charlotte, peeled and cut lengthways into 5-mm-thick slices

6 garlic cloves, sliced

2 large courgettes (350 g), sliced

1 large aubergine (350 g), cut into 1-cm-thick slices

1 large green pepper, seeded and cut into chunks

1 large red pepper, seeded and cut into chunks

1 large red onion, halved and thickly sliced

15–20 g dill sprigs

15–20 g flat-leaf parsley sprigs

2 large beef tomatoes, woody cores removed, thickly sliced

200 ml sieved canned tomatoes, such as passata

Salt and freshly ground black pepper

Preheat the oven to 190°C/Gas Mark 5. In a large (about 26 x 36 cm) well-oiled roasting tin, spread the potatoes out in a single layer. Season with salt and pepper, then scatter over the garlic and courgettes. Season once more, then add a layer each of the aubergine, green peppers, red peppers and then red onion, continuing to season between each layer. Scatter over half of the dill and parsley sprigs, cover with the tomato slices and then add the rest of the dill and parsley and a final seasoning. Pour the sieved tomatoes over the top, followed by the olive oil.

Cover the roasting tin tightly with foil and bake for approximately 1½ hours. If the vegetables have released a lot of juices, carefully pour them off into a wide pan and boil rapidly until nicely concentrated in flavour. Pour back over the vegetables and leave to cool slightly before serving.

Kanoi, Corfu

IN MY EARLY DAYS of travelling to Greece, we soon started to notice that they like to serve their food cold, and stuffed tomatoes is a dish that particularly comes to mind in this respect. Walking into a kitchen somewhere in the Peloponnese, we would choose a lunch of cold stuffed tomatoes, dolmades, beans in tomato sauce, fish *plaki* (baked) or moussaka. But actually, thinking about it, not moussaka, because it was always, 'Oh, not today, tomorrow moussaka.' What's the Greek word for tomorrow? *Avrio*? That's like saying *mañana*. But in the end I learnt that I was missing the point. Their food is not cold, it's lukewarm, and that's how they like to serve things like a good stuffed tomato because then you can taste all the flavours so much better. This recipe is simple but works, even with our slightly insipid British tomatoes. The important points to note for making good ones are to reduce the tomato pulp down well with the garlic and onion and then make a well-flavoured pilaf rice with some good chicken stock, adding lots of fresh herbs at the end. Serve with some chips fried in olive oil and a crisp green salad. *Serves 6*

TOMATAKIA GEMISTA:
BAKED TOMATOES STUFFED WITH RICE, PINE NUTS AND KEFALOTIRI CHEESE
CORFU

12 large beef tomatoes, such as Jack Hawkins or Marmande, each weighing about 250 g
½ teaspoon sugar
200 ml extra virgin olive oil
2 garlic cloves, finely chopped
2 medium onions, finely chopped
200 g long grain rice

400 ml well-flavoured *Chicken stock* (see page 211)
50 g lightly toasted pine nuts
2 tablespoons chopped mint
2 tablespoons chopped parsley
50 g finely grated Greek kefalotiri cheese or parmesan cheese
Salt and freshly ground black pepper

Preheat the oven to 180°C/Gas Mark 4. Take a 2-cm slice off the rounded top of each tomato. Scoop out the pulp from the inside of the tomato and the lid and roughly chop, saving all the juices.

Sprinkle the inside of the tomatoes and the lids with a little salt, pepper and a pinch of sugar. Pack the tomatoes close together into a shallow ovenproof dish.

For the stuffing, heat 100 ml of the olive oil in a saucepan, add the garlic and onion and cook gently for about 10 minutes until soft and lightly browned. Add the tomato pulp and juices and leave to simmer quite vigorously, stirring every now and then, until it is reduced and concentrated in flavour.

Stir in the rice and stock, season with 2 teaspoons salt and plenty of freshly ground pepper, bring to the boil, cover and simmer for 15 minutes. The rice will only be part-cooked at this stage. Stir in the toasted pine nuts, chopped mint, parsley and grated cheese.

Spoon the rice mixture into the tomatoes, leaving some room at the top for the rice to expand, cover them with the lids and pour over the remaining oil. Bake for 60–80 minutes until the tomatoes are very tender – this will depend on the variety of tomato that you use.

I HAVE A NEW and what I suspect will be an everlasting affection for Moroccan salads. This one comes from the El Minzah hotel in Tangiers. Normally we don't stay in deluxe hotels when we are filming because the budget won't allow it, but we all loved the El Minzah. It is situated right above the Grand Socco, the ancient market, and right at the entrance of the medina, the old walled city of Tangiers, and has great views over the port and the Straits of Gibraltar. Like so many Moroccan homes and riads, it has been built round a peaceful blue-and-white-tiled courtyard with a fountain trickling away in the centre. It reminded me of the way Raffles Hotel in Singapore used to be: a little worn by time, not a hundred per cent efficient but not expensive, gloriously comfortable and atmospheric. This salad is the perfect accompaniment to the mechoui lamb on page 132. *Serves 6–8*

TOMATO, ROASTED RED PEPPER AND ONION SALAD WITH PRESERVED LEMON
MOROCCO

2 red peppers

500 g ripe and juicy tomatoes, skinned

1 small red onion, finely chopped

60 g *Preserved lemon* (see page 209), flesh removed and discarded and the skin chopped into small pieces

2 tablespoons chopped fresh coriander

For the dressing

1½ tablespoons lemon juice

3 tablespoons extra virgin olive oil

1 medium-hot red chilli, seeded and finely chopped

1 garlic clove, finely chopped

Salt and freshly ground black pepper

Roast the red peppers in a preheated 220°C/Gas 7 oven for 20 minutes, turning them once. Seal them in a plastic bag and leave to cool. Then break them open, discard the stalk, seeds and skin and cut the flesh into short chunky strips.

Skin the tomatoes, halve and deseed them and then cut them into small, chunky pieces. Scatter them over the base of a serving platter. Scatter over the red peppers, followed by the red onion and the preserved lemon.

Just before serving, whisk the lemon juice and olive oil together and stir in the red chilli, garlic and some salt and pepper to taste. Drizzle the dressing over the salad, sprinkle over the chopped coriander and serve.

THIS IS FROM from Sam and Eddie Hart's *Modern Spanish Cooking*. They cooked it for me at their house in Estellencs south of Deià, on the west coast of Mallorca. I've known Sam and Eddie for a long time and watched their two tapas bars in London, Fino and Barrafina, go from strength to strength. *Serves 6 as a side dish*

TUMBET:
OVEN-BAKED POTATOES, PEPPERS, TOMATOES AND ONIONS
MALLORCA

For the tumbet

2 large aubergines (about 750 g), stalk ends removed

1 kg floury potatoes, such as Maris Piper

About 10 tablespoons extra virgin olive oil

2 large red peppers

Sea salt and freshly ground black pepper

For the tomato sauce

14 plum tomatoes (about 1.5 kg)

2–3 tablespoons extra virgin olive oil

½ onion, chopped

1 banana shallot, or 3 ordinary shallots, finely chopped

2 garlic cloves, thinly sliced

1 large thyme sprig

1 oregano sprig

2 bay leaves

For the tumbet, cut the aubergines across into 1.5-cm thick rounds and lay them out on kitchen paper. Sprinkle liberally with salt and leave to degorge (draw out the juices) for about 20 minutes.

Peel the potatoes and cut into 5-mm-thick rounds. Heat 2 tablespoons of the olive oil in a large frying pan over a medium heat and fry the potato slices in batches for about 10 minutes on each side until golden brown and tender. Season lightly with salt and pepper and put to one side. (You may need to add a little more oil as you fry each batch.)

Halve, core and deseed the peppers, then slice lengthways into 1-cm strips. Heat another 2 tablespoons of the olive oil in the pan and fry the peppers over a medium heat for 20–25 minutes, stirring occasionally. Remove, season lightly and set aside.

Meanwhile, pat the aubergine slices dry with kitchen paper to remove the salt and juices. Heat another 2 tablespoons of olive oil in another large frying pan and fry the aubergine slices in batches, until golden brown on both sides, adding more oil as necessary with each batch. Set aside.

To make the tomato sauce, briefly immerse the tomatoes in boiling water to loosen the skins. Peel the tomatoes, quarter and remove the seeds. Heat the olive oil in a large frying pan over a medium heat. Add the onion and shallot and sweat for 15 minutes. Add the garlic, thyme, oregano and bay leaves and sweat for a further 5 minutes. Add the tomatoes, bring to a simmer and reduce slowly for 25–30 minutes to a thickish sauce. Remove and discard the bay leaves and thyme and oregano stalks, and season to taste.

To bake the tumbet, preheat the oven to 190°C/Gas Mark 5. Oil the base and sides of a shallow earthenware (or other) ovenproof dish. Lay the potato slices over the bottom of the dish. Cover with the red pepper strips, then a layer of aubergines on top. Pour the tomato sauce over the top of the dish and bake for 25–30 minutes. Serve immediately.

YOU CAN OFTEN pick up a recipe and turn out a very truthful rendition of a dish, even if you have never tasted the original. Caponata is not such a dish – which I discovered only after I'd tasted the perfect one in Sciacca in Sicily. We had been there to taste the anchovies in olive oil; the owner had taken us around and pointed out that the best anchovies have to be cleaned, filleted and salted the day they are caught. We were very impressed with Angostino Recca. He had spent a large part of his life in New York working in various unspecified businesses and had a voice just like Marlon Brando in *The Godfather*. Just as we were leaving, his wife produced a plate of caponata, and then I realized how the dish worked. It should be tart and sweet but not too much of either, the celery should be firm but not too crunchy and there should be plenty of pleasingly soft but not mushy aubergines. I think of it as more of an Italian relish, and it goes well with prosciutto, grilled fish or grilled chicken. *Serves 6–8 as a side dish or antipasto*

CAPONATA:

SWEET AND SOUR AUBERGINE RELISH WITH TOMATOES, CELERY, CAPERS AND OLIVES

SICILY

4 medium-sized aubergines (about 1 kg)

150 ml extra virgin olive oil

1 medium onion, chopped

3 celery sticks, cut into 1-cm pieces

4 tablespoons red wine vinegar

400-g can chopped tomatoes

2 tablespoons caster sugar

1 tablespoon drained capers, rinsed

75 g pitted green olives, quartered lengthways

Salt and freshly ground black pepper

Cut the aubergines into 1.5-cm chunks, place in a colander with 2 teaspoons of salt and toss together well. Leave to drain for 30–40 minutes.

Pat the aubergines dry with kitchen paper to remove the salt and juices. Heat half the oil in a large, wide-based pan, add the aubergines and fry until tender but still holding their shape. Lift out and set aside.

Add the remaining oil to the pan with the onion and cook gently for 10 minutes until soft and lightly browned. Add the celery and cook for 5 minutes.

Add the vinegar and leave it to bubble away until it has almost disappeared. Add the tomatoes, sugar, ½ teaspoon salt and 20 turns of the black pepper mill. Cover and leave to simmer for 20 minutes until the celery is tender. Uncover and stir in the capers, green olives and aubergines and adjust the seasoning if necessary. Serve warm or cold.

THIS SOUP SAYS a lot about the cooking of Corsica. I first went there in the mid-1980s expecting lots of Provençal-style fish dishes and was a tad disappointed. I was staying on the coast but soon realized that I should have spent more time inland, particularly up in the mountains. On my recent trip there I did just that and this romantic soup, full of the smoky flavour of mountain ham and the herbs of the maquis, the dense shrub that covers much of the island, is one of the best dishes I tried. It was at the Juillard sisters' famous *ferme d'auberge* near the town of Murato. The marvel of Corsican food is the quality of the ingredients, and a visit to their restaurant is a must, because real Corsican food is ruggedly rural. It's almost impossible, here in the UK, to get the air-dried mountain ham cured in an open chimney like you would in Corsica, so I've used a smoked ham hock instead. *Serves 8–10 generously*

MINESTRA:
CORSICAN VEGETABLE SOUP WITH SMOKED HAM, CABBAGE AND BORLOTTI BEANS
CORSICA

3 tablespoons extra virgin olive oil, plus extra for serving

1 large onion, chopped

5 garlic cloves, thinly sliced

1 large leek, cleaned and cut into similar-sized pieces

250 g dried borlotti beans, soaked overnight

450 g waxy potatoes, such as Charlotte, peeled and cut into 1-cm dice

250 g peeled carrots, cut into 1-cm dice

2 celery sticks, cut into 1-cm dice

1 ripe beef tomato, skinned and chopped

Leaves from 1 small rosemary sprig, finely chopped

½ teaspoon dried oregano

1.2 kg smoked ham hock

250 g green beans, trimmed and cut into 1-cm pieces

2 medium-sized courgettes, topped and tailed and cut into 1-cm dice

½ small cabbage (about 500 g), core removed, thinly sliced

75 g dried tagliatelle, broken into 5-cm pieces

1 tablespoon chopped fresh oregano

A small handful of flat-leaf parsley leaves, chopped

Salt and freshly ground black pepper

Heat the oil in a really large pan, add the onion, garlic and leek, and cook gently for 3–4 minutes. Drain the soaked beans and add to the pan with the potatoes, carrots, celery, tomato, rosemary, dried oregano and 2 litres water. Cut the ham hock in half lengthways to one side of the bone, add to the pan and press the pieces down well into the soup so they are totally submerged. Bring everything to a simmer and leave to cook, uncovered, for 1 hour.

Then add the green beans, courgettes, cabbage, tagliatelle pieces and fresh oregano and simmer for a further 15–20 minutes until the soup is thick. Remove the pieces of ham hock, pull the meat off the bone, and pull it into small chunks. Discard the skin and bone. Stir the ham back into the soup with the parsley and approximately 500 ml more hot water to loosen it slightly and season to taste with salt and pepper. Serve in large warmed soup bowls, drizzled with a little more olive oil.

ONE OF MY ENDURING memories of my first trip to Turkey, many years ago, was being woken by the muezzin calling the locals to prayer at the Blue Mosque in Istanbul. It's something that seems strange to start with, but then you soon look forward to it, even at three o'clock in the morning when you're not sleeping. I liked the contemplative atmosphere in the mosque: no furniture, just the blue tiles on the walls, and the often beautiful carpets on the stone floor. Driving through Turkey, you become accustomed to picking out villages in the distance by the spindly minarets rising into the sky: they become a friendly landmark, like church towers but different. This recipe is from Claudia Roden's evocative book *Arabesque*. The joke about the name is well known. It means 'the Imam fainted', either because the priest was so overwhelmed by the flavour of the dish cooked for him by his wife, or because he was broken by the expense of the large amount of olive oil used in the cooking of it. Whichever it is, this is vegetarian cooking at its best. Serve at room temperature. *Serves 6*

IMAM BAYILDI:
AUBERGINES STUFFED WITH FRIED ONIONS, TOMATO, CHILLI AND PARSLEY

TURKEY

6 aubergines, each weighing about 250 g

200 ml extra virgin olive oil

2 medium onions, halved and thinly sliced

5 garlic cloves, finely chopped

1 medium-hot red chilli, seeded and chopped (optional)

½ teaspoon Aleppo pepper (see page 207)

225-g can chopped tomatoes, or 4 very

ripe tomatoes, skinned and chopped

1 heaped teaspoon *Turkish red pepper paste* (see page 209)

25 g chopped flat-leaf parsley leaves

250 ml good quality tomato juice

1 teaspoon caster sugar

Juice ½ lemon

Salt and freshly ground black pepper

Using a potato peeler and working lengthways, peel away 1-cm-wide strips of skin to leave the aubergines striped in appearance. Now cut a long, narrow wedge out of each aubergine to make a deep pocket, taking care not to cut all the way through to the other side, or at either end. Sprinkle a little salt into each pocket and leave them to drain, upside down, for 30–40 minutes.

Heat the 4 tablespoons of oil in the frying pan. Add the onions and fry gently for 10 minutes until soft but not browned. Add the garlic, chilli and Aleppo pepper and fry gently for another 5 minutes. Remove from the heat and stir in the tomatoes, Turkish red pepper paste, parsley and seasoning to taste. Spoon the filling into the aubergines and put them, side by side and slit-side up, in a wide shallow saucepan.

Mix the tomato juice with the sugar, lemon juice, ½ teaspoon salt and some freshly ground black pepper. Pour over the aubergines, followed by the remaining oil. Cover and simmer gently for 40 minutes until the aubergines are tender. If the sauce is still quite thin, uncover, increase the heat slightly and simmer more vigorously for about 10 minutes, moving them gently every now and then to prevent them from sticking, until the liquid has reduced and just a few tablespoons remain. Spoon away some of the excess oil if you wish.

THIS RECIPE comes from a friend of mine, Matthew Drennan, the editor of *Delicious* magazine. It's light and fresh; the dressing is quite lemony and goes well with the saltiness of the prosciutto and Parmesan cheese. And the dressing, of course, stops the raw artichoke hearts from discolouring. Make sure you use young artichokes, keep them in acidulated water and shave them on the mandolin straight into the dressing at the last minute: this isn't a salad that can wait. The true texture and flavour of artichokes is something I only discovered on my travels in the Mediterranean. This is the sort of light first course I'm always looking for in restaurants. *Serves 4*

ARTICHOKE
AND PROSCIUTTO SALAD WITH ROCKET
PUGLIA

3 tablespoons extra virgin olive oil

Juice 2 lemons

4 large globe artichokes

100 g thinly sliced prosciutto (air-dried ham, such as parma)

25 g wild rocket leaves

50-g piece parmesan cheese

Salt and freshly ground black pepper

First make the dressing so it is ready for the artichokes as soon as they are prepared. Put the olive oil, 2 tablespoons of the lemon juice and plenty of seasoning into a large bowl and whisk together well. Set aside.

To prepare the artichokes, cut off the top half and the stalk, then slice away the dark green outer leaves, exposing the lighter green and tender part. Drop the artichoke bases into a pan of acidulated water (water and the remaining lemon juice) to prevent them going brown.

Just before serving, arrange the slices of prosciutto over the base of 4 plates. Very thinly slice the artichoke bases across, ideally using a mandolin, straight into the dressing and immediately toss them together to avoid any discolouration.

Scatter the dressed artichokes on top of the prosciutto and then loosely scatter over the rocket leaves. Thinly shave over the parmesan cheese and serve straight away.

THE RECIPE comes from the River Restaurant in Lefkimmi, just north of Kavos. The family who run this vegetarian restaurant are single-minded in producing only the sort of vegetable dishes that the Greeks eat at home, dishes that can be hard to find on the island. The son, Yanni, told me how delighted he was to be back working with his parents. He had spent years in Kavos, serving food up to largely British package tours, who he said would never have wanted to eat anything like this. This, a sort of vegetable stew, is the type of Greek cooking I adore. Don't worry about losing the bright greenness of the peas. The amalgamation of peas, artichokes, lemon, olive oil and dill is unusual for us and yet so typically Greek. Loula thickened the stew slightly with some flour but I prefer to leave it just as it is, naturally thickened by the olive oil forming an emulsion with the lemon juice. At home, for a special lunch, Greeks tend to serve everything on the table at the same time. So a dish like this might come with kleftiko (see the recipe on page 131), briam (see page 54), a Greek salad (see page 70), maybe stuffed tomatoes (see page 56) or peppers and perhaps some beans in a tomato sauce (see page 176). *Serves 6*

BRAISED ARTICHOKES
WITH PEAS AND DILL
CORFU

6 medium-sized globe artichokes

Juice ½ lemon

150 ml extra virgin olive oil

1 large onion, halved and thinly sliced

2 garlic cloves, crushed

175 g fresh or frozen peas

20 g dill sprigs, roughly chopped

Salt and freshly ground black pepper

To prepare the artichokes, cut off the top half and the stalk, then slice away the dark green outer leaves, exposing the lighter green and tender part.

In a shallow, flameproof casserole dish or wide-based pan, heat the olive oil, add the onions and garlic and cook until soft but not browned – about 10 minutes.

Add the artichoke hearts to the pan, cover and cook for 5 minutes. Uncover, add the peas, 100 ml water, the lemon juice, half the dill, 1 teaspoon salt and some pepper and cook for a further 6–8 minutes until the artichokes are tender and the oil has formed an emulsion with the water and lemon juice. Add the rest of the dill, adjust the seasoning if necessary and serve.

Morocco

THIS RECIPE is based on a carrot salad I had at the Hotel Arabesque in the medina of Fes. Morocco has brought a whole new world of possibilities with vegetable salads to my repertoire. The idea of tender cooked carrots served with a fresh dressing of olive oil, lemon juice, orange flower and mint is very exotic. The salad can be made with coarsely grated raw carrots too. *Serves 4*

CARROT SALAD
WITH ORANGE FLOWER WATER AND MINT
MOROCCO

600 g medium-sized carrots, peeled

1 tablespoon good quality orange flower water

½ garlic clove, very finely chopped

½ teaspoon caster sugar

1½ tablespoons lemon juice

2 tablespoons extra virgin olive oil

1 tablespoon chopped mint

Salt

Cut the carrots into triangular shaped chunks along their length. Drop them into a pan of boiling salted water and cook for 6–7 minutes until just tender. Drain and leave to cool slightly.

Combine the orange flower water, garlic, sugar, lemon juice and oil together in a small bowl and toss through the salad. Just before serving stir the mint through, and serve at room temperature.

THE MOROCCANS have an enduring affection for beetroot. It seems very much a northern European vegetable to me, not one from hot and hazy Morocco, but they certainly know how to turn it out well. This salad, made with preserved lemon, olive oil and a pinch of cinnamon, is a delight, and is another typical kemia-style dish (see the recipe for chakchouka on page 33). As with many Moroccan salads, the beetroot can also be dressed with a little orange flower water, or can be mixed with some sliced oranges and served dressed with a little olive oil, a pinch of sugar and some lightly toasted walnuts. *Serves 4*

BEETROOT SALAD
WITH CINNAMON AND PRESERVED LEMON
MOROCCO

500 g large beetroot, scrubbed clean

1 tablespoon caster sugar

Juice 1 lemon

1 tablespoon olive oil

A large pinch of freshly ground cinnamon

60 g *Preserved lemon* (see page 209), flesh removed and discarded and the skin chopped into small pieces

1 tablespoon chopped flat-leaf parsley

Salt

Put the beetroot into a pan of cold water, bring to the boil and simmer for 1–1½ hours until tender. Drain, leave to cool, and then slip off their skins.

Cut the beetroot into 1.5-cm chunks. Mix with the sugar, lemon juice, olive oil, cinnamon, preserved lemon and ½ teaspoon salt. Set aside for 1 hour. Stir in the parsley, adjust the seasoning if necessary and serve at room temperature.

PECORINO

FETA

RICOTTA

MOZZARELLA

RUGGED CHEESES ARE AS CHARACTERISTIC
OF THE REGION AS THE OLIVE, THE CAPER
AND THE ANCHOVY

Torrent de Parlos, northern Mallorca

NEAR WHERE THE FERRIES dock in Corfu town is a restaurant called Bekios, which was filled with locals and had an intriguingly misspelled English menu, typical of all the best places in Greece. But then I say to myself: When you've finished laughing, try writing your own menu in Greek. We went there virtually every night because we liked the locals. They are friendly to each other, take all their kids with them, and, as a race, seem content with their lot. We drank retsina of course and, above all, marvelled at the perfection of the horiatiki salad. It's all about the quality of the feta and the olives, I think, with just a sprinkling of dried oregano over the top. *Serves 4*

SALATA HORIATIKI:
GREEK SALAD WITH TOMATO, CUCUMBER, OLIVES, DILL AND FETA CHEESE
CORFU

450 g ripe, red, well-flavoured tomatoes

½ cucumber

1 red onion

200 g Greek feta cheese

4½ tablespoons extra virgin olive oil, plus a little extra to serve

1 tablespoon red wine vinegar

1 teaspoon ouzo or Pernod

2 tablespoons chopped dill

20 small black olives

Large pinch of dried oregano, Greek if possible

Salt and freshly ground black pepper

Crusty fresh bread, to serve

Cut the tomatoes into chunks, and cut the cucumber in half lengthways and then across into thick slices. Very thinly slice the red onion. Crumble the feta cheese into small chunks.

Put the olive oil, ½ teaspoon salt, the red wine vinegar, ouzo and some black pepper into a large salad bowl and whisk together. Add the tomatoes, cucumber and onions and toss together gently. Add the feta cheese, chopped dill and olives and mix briefly, then divide between 4 plates.

Drizzle the salad with a little more olive oil, sprinkle with the dried oregano and a little coarsely ground black pepper, and serve with some crusty fresh bread.

THIS RECIPE COMES from Il Frantoio, a restaurant in a masseria near Ostuni. It's on an enormous estate mainly made up of olive groves, beautifully situated with hills on one side and the sea on the other. This was the main dish of Easter Sunday lunch. The combination of the two cheeses with the tomato and lamb made it rich but irresistible. I rang Debbie from Puglia and asked her to test it for me. She had to cook it for her parents twice, they liked it so much. And with it I remember we drank an exquisite Primitivo called Visellio, from a winemaker called Tenute Rubino, which had a lovely tobaccoey flavour. Another dish I remember from this seven- or eight-course banquet lunch was of wild herbs gathered on the estate with tomato, garlic, olive oil, pecorino and Parmesan and some little meatballs, all cooked in a vegetable broth. I went out after lunch with one of the waiters, who was an expert in gathering these wild chicories, thistles, asparagus and even poppies and mallows. Both here and in Corfu (see page 48) they are serious about gathering wild greens. *Serves 6*

EASTER LAMB
BAKED WITH PECORINO, POTATO, TOMATOES AND GARLIC
PUGLIA

1.25 kg boneless leg of spring lamb

5 tablespoons extra virgin olive oil

750–800 g peeled floury potatoes, such as
   Maris Piper, cut into 5-mm-thick slices

375 g small, vine-ripened tomatoes, halved

The leaves from 20g flat-leaf parsley, chopped

3 large cloves garlic, chopped

50 g finely grated pecorino cheese

50 g finely grated parmesan cheese

Salt and freshly ground black pepper

Preheat the oven to 180°C/Gas Mark 4. Trim the lamb of excess fat and cut the meat into 4-cm cubes. Take a casserole dish that's about 24 cm wide and 9–10 cm high. Pour 2 tablespoons of the olive oil into it and spread one third of the potatoes over the base. Season with some salt and pepper, then scatter over half the meat and season once more.

Squeeze the tomatoes over the sink to rid them of their seeds, then thickly slice. Scatter half the tomatoes, parsley and garlic over the lamb, season and then sprinkle with half the cheese and another tablespoon of the olive oil.

Now add another one third of the potatoes, the rest of the meat and some seasoning followed by the rest of the tomatoes, parsley, garlic and a little more seasoning. Cover with the remaining potatoes, season for the last time and sprinkle with the remaining cheese and olive oil.

Cover and bake in the oven for 30 minutes. Then uncover and bake for a further 1 hour until the lamb and potatoes are tender and everything is covered in a golden, cheesy crust.

THE NAME FOR this classic Italian sandwich is 'mozzarella in a carriage', the carriage being the bread. It's important to use a cheese with good melting qualities, so in this case use the basic cow's milk mozzarella rather than the more expensive one made from buffalo milk, which with its superior texture is better served on its own. When Debbie and I were testing this recipe and deciding whether or not to add another piece of parma ham while exclaiming how good they were, I suddenly had a mighty thirst for a bottle of Chalky's Bite. This is a beer we developed with a local brewery in Cornwall called Sharps. It's a Belgian style of beer – strong, hoppy but light in colour – to which we've added a trace of Cornish wild fennel, and it is named after my sadly departed dog. The beer is designed to be drunk with food, and in a flash of inspiration I thought that the fried bread filled with cheese and ham would be the perfect accompaniment to a slightly punchy beer like this – and so it was. Needless to say this beer is on my website if you'd like a case or two! Serve the hot sandwich with a dressed mixed-leaf salad if you wish. *Makes 6*

MOZZARELLA IN CARROZZA:
A HOT SANDWICH OF MOZZARELLA CHEESE, ANCHOVY AND PARMA HAM
SICILY

12 thin slices of fresh white bread, taken
   from a tin-shaped loaf
25 g softened butter
6 thin slices of prosciutto (air-dried ham,
   such as parma)
2 x 150-g mozzarella cheeses, drained and
   each cut into 6 thin slices

3 anchovy fillets in olive oil, drained and
   halved
25 g plain flour
2 eggs, beaten
100 g fresh white breadcrumbs
A mixture of olive and sunflower oil,
   for shallow-frying

Lay 6 slices of the bread on a chopping board and spread lightly with the butter. Cut each slice of prosciutto in half and place one piece in the centre of each one. Top with two thin slices of mozzarella cheese and then cover with the second piece of ham and one piece of anchovy fillet. Cover with the remaining slices of bread and press together well. Then, using a 9.5-cm plain cutter, or a ramekin as a guide, cut round the cheese to make 6 little sandwiches.

Put the flour, beaten eggs and breadcrumbs into 3 separate shallow dishes. Dip the sandwiches one at a time into the flour, then the egg and finally the breadcrumbs, pressing them down well to make sure they take on a thick, even coating. Roll the edges of the sandwiches once more in egg and breadcrumbs to make a good seal.

Pour the olive and sunflower oil into a large, deep frying pan to a depth of 1 cm and heat to 180°C. Fry the sandwiches in batches for 1½ minutes on each side until crisp and golden. Drain on kitchen paper and serve warm.

SPAGHETTI ALLA CARBONARA:

PASTA WITH PECORINO SARDO, PANCETTA, PARSLEY AND EGGS

SARDINIA

I WAS A LITTLE SHAMED last year watching an Italian chef in Australia, Steve Manfredi, talking on a cookery programme about carbonara. 'Never,' he said, 'would the Romans dream of putting anything but pecorino romano in it, and adding cream is unforgivable.' Until that time I had been cheerfully using both parmesan and cream. But I think he was right. Since then I have found the dish much more characterful, curiously reminiscent of pasta dishes on Greek ferries, where they tend to use kefalotiri cheese rather than parmesan. But I must say, using mature Sardinian pecorino is a step even further in the direction of punchy flavour. *Serves 4*

400 g dried spaghetti

175-g piece smoked pancetta, rind removed

2 tablespoons extra virgin olive oil

3 garlic cloves, finely chopped

A handful of flat-leaf parsley leaves, finely chopped

3 large eggs, beaten

50 g finely grated pecorino sardo maturo

Salt and freshly ground black pepper

Bring 4.5 litres water to the boil in a large saucepan with 8 teaspoons salt. Add the spaghetti and cook for 9 minutes or until *al dente*.

Meanwhile, cut the pancetta into lardons (short little strips), about 6 mm wide. Heat a large, deep frying pan over a medium-high heat, add the oil and the pancetta and allow it to fry until lightly golden. Add the garlic and parsley and cook for a few seconds, then remove from the heat and set to one side.

Drain the spaghetti well, tip into the frying pan with the pancetta, garlic and parsley, add the beaten eggs and half the grated pecorino cheese and toss together well. Season to taste with a little salt and black pepper. The heat from the spaghetti will be sufficient to partly cook the egg but still leave it moist and creamy. Take to the table and serve in warmed pasta bowls, sprinkled with the rest of the cheese.

Alghero, Sardinia

THIS IS A DISH from a chef at the Seafood Restaurant, Paul Rowley, who worked for me for a few years and now works for my previous executive chef, Roy Brett, as head chef at the Dakota hotel and restaurant at Forth Bridge. Its success lies in the quality of the homemade pasta made with plenty of eggs, and the combination of fresh basil, spinach and good ricotta, one of the most revered cheeses of the island. It's a cheffy dish – everything has to be assembled at the last minute – and it's quite tricky to keep everything warm while you do so, but it's worth it. I've added a pinch of pecorino to give the dish a little lift. *Serves 4*

FRESH PAPPARDELLE
WITH RICOTTA, SPINACH, BASIL AND LEMON
SICILY

7 tablespoons extra virgin olive oil, plus a little extra for the pasta

150 g fresh ricotta, drained overnight in a sieve if from a tub

350 g baby leaf spinach, washed, drained and large stalks removed

Leaves from 1 large pot of basil

1 teaspoon lemon juice

Sea salt flakes and freshly ground black pepper

Finely grated pecorino or parmesan cheese, to serve

For the pasta

225 g plain flour

1½ teaspoons extra virgin olive oil

4 medium egg yolks

2 medium eggs

½ teaspoon salt

For the pasta, put all the ingredients into a food processor and blend until they come together into a dough. Tip out onto a work surface and knead for about 10 minutes until smooth and elastic. Wrap in clingfilm and leave to rest for 10–15 minutes. Cut the pasta dough into 4 even-sized pieces and roll out one at a time using a pasta machine (follow the maker's instructions), finishing on setting number 5. Lightly dust each piece in turn with flour, lay it out flat and neatly trim the edges. Cut each piece into 20-cm lengths and then cut lengthways into 2-cm-wide strips. Set aside on a floured surface while you roll out and cut the rest.

Bring 4.5 litres water to the boil in a large saucepan with 8 teaspoons salt.

Gently warm 4 tablespoons of the oil in a small, shallow pan. Carefully break the ricotta into small chunks, add them to the oil and leave over a very low heat to warm through. Heat the remaining oil in a medium-sized pan, add the spinach a handful at a time and cook until it has all wilted down. Add the basil leaves, fold them through the spinach with the lemon juice and season to taste with salt and pepper. Keep warm.

Drop the pasta into the water and cook for 1 minute. Drain well, return to the pan and toss with a little oil to stop the strips from sticking together.

To serve, arrange the pappardelle (about 7–8 strips per person) with spoonfuls of the warmed ricotta and the spinach mixture attractively in 4 warm, shallow pasta bowls, finishing with some of the ricotta and spinach on top. Drizzle with a little of the oil from the ricotta and sprinkle with some coarsely ground black pepper, a few sea salt flakes and a little finely grated cheese.

I SUPPOSE the simplest way of describing a calzone is as a pizza shaped into a pasty-like turnover. The classic filling is salami, ham and cheese, but I've added a bit of well-reduced tomato sauce too. When it comes out hot from the oven the filling is runny and intensely flavoured, but the way it sinks into the bread and flavours it is what a calzone is all about. The amount of dough for six might seem a bit mean, but the object is to force you to roll the discs out as thinly as possible, so that the finished bread casing isn't too thick. Unless you have a huge oven, these pizzas have to be made and cooked in batches, but they lend themselves perfectly to a friendly, informal way of eating. *Makes 6*

CALZONE:
CLOSED PIZZA WITH TOMATO, SALAMI, HAM AND MOZZARELLA CHEESE
PUGLIA

4 rounded tablespoons *Tomato sauce* (see page 211)

2 x 150-g mozzarella cheeses, drained and cut into 1-cm dice

75 g piece **Napoli salami**, skinned and cut into 5-mm dice

75 g piece thickly sliced ham, cut into 5-mm dice

Freshly ground black pepper

For the dough

550 g strong white flour, plus extra for dusting

3 teaspoons easy-blend yeast

2 teaspoons salt

350 ml hand-hot water

4 teaspoons olive oil

4 teaspoons polenta or semolina

For the dough, sift the flour, yeast and salt into a bowl and make a dip in the centre. Add the warm water and olive oil and mix the two together into a soft dough. Tip out onto a lightly floured surface and knead for 5 minutes. Then return to the bowl, cover with clingfilm and leave somewhere warm for approximately 1 hour or until doubled in size.

Preheat the oven to 220°C/Gas Mark 7. Knock the air out of the dough, turn it out onto a lightly floured surface and knead it briefly once more until smooth. Divide into 6 pieces and keep the spare ones covered with clingfilm while you shape the first pizza.

Mix the tomato sauce with the mozzarella cheese, salami and ham in a bowl and season with 20 turns of the black pepper mill. Lightly sprinkle a baking sheet with a little polenta or semolina. Roll one piece of dough out into a disc approximately 23 cm in diameter, lift it onto the baking sheet and reshape it with your fingers into a round. Spread one sixth of the filling onto one half of the disc, taking it to within about 2.5 cm of the edge. Moisten one half of the edge with a little water and fold the other side of the dough over the filling so that the edges meet. Press them together well to make a good seal and dust the top with a little flour. Repeat to make a second pizza.

Bake the pizzas for 20 minutes until crisp and golden. Meanwhile, shape another 2 pizzas on another baking sheet. Bake as before while shaping the last 2 pizzas. Remove the pizzas from the oven as soon as they are cooked and serve immediately.

YOU MIGHT ASK what is so special about my *parmigiana di melanzana*. It's all about the balance. Not too much tomato sauce, but a little of a well-reduced and well-flavoured one, the use of taleggio cheese, which is slightly richer than the more usual mozzarella, plenty of basil otherwise the flavour is too faint, and not too long a cooking time so that the aubergines still taste of aubergines. As I've said before, good vegetarian cooking is not about cooking for non-meat eaters. This seems to me to be a perfectly balanced combination of flavours that simply doesn't need meat or fish. *Serves 6*

PARMIGIANA DI MELANZANA:
BAKED SLICED AUBERGINES WITH TOMATO, TALEGGIO AND PARMESAN CHEESE
PUGLIA

1 kg aubergines

150 ml extra virgin olive oil

200 g taleggio cheese

24 fresh basil leaves, finely shredded

½ quantity *Tomato sauce* (see page 211)

50 g finely grated parmesan cheese

Salt

Top and tail the aubergines and slice them lengthways into 1-cm-thick slices. Sprinkle them lightly with salt and leave them layered up in a colander to drain for 30–40 minutes. This will help to stop them from absorbing too much oil.

Preheat the oven to 200°C/Gas Mark 6. Pat the aubergines dry with kitchen paper to remove the salt and juices. Heat about 2 tablespoons of the oil in a large frying pan, add a layer of aubergine slices and fry them over a medium heat for about 2 minutes on each side until tender and nicely golden. Set aside on a plate and repeat with the remaining aubergines.

Cut the piece of taleggio in half (between the two rinded sides) and then cut each piece into long, thin slices, using another sharp knife to help you slide them off the blade if necessary.

To assemble the dish, lay half the aubergine slices over the base of a 20 x 30-cm shallow oven-proof dish. Scatter over the basil and then spread over half of the tomato sauce. Cover with half of the taleggio slices and then sprinkle with half of the parmesan. Repeat the layers once more. Bake for 20 minutes until bubbling hot.

SARDINES
RED MULLET
SWORDFISH
CALAMARI TUNA

RECIPES FOR ALL
THOSE MEDITERRANEAN
FISH THAT I LOVE

THE ETANG DE DIANE on the eastern coast of Corsica has been famous for its oysters since Roman times. They are extremely good and I polished off a dozen or so in the market in Bastia. We didn't make it to Aléria, the historical capital of the island, close to the lake, but I wrote this recipe with those big, juicy, salty oysters in mind. While generally I prefer my oysters *au nature* – that is, with no more than a squeeze of lemon juice – there are times when a little delicate flavouring to a raw oyster is very pleasurable. I'm thinking here particularly of a drinks party. Oriental combinations of soy sauce, ginger, spring onions and so on are most acceptable but there's an interesting trend evolving in Mediterranean cooking for serving raw or marinated seafood or fish with the flavours of olive oil and lemon juice. Here I've also added a note of aniseed with the addition of Pernod and tarragon. *Serves 4*

OYSTERS
WITH A PERNOD, SHALLOT, TARRAGON AND OLIVE OIL DRESSING
CORSICA

20 oysters

2 small shallots, finely chopped

½ tablespoon roughly chopped tarragon

½ tablespoon roughly chopped flat-leaf parsley

1 teaspoon Dijon mustard

1 teaspoon dark soy sauce

5 tablespoons extra virgin olive oil

1½ tablespoons freshly squeezed lemon juice

1 teaspoon Pernod

Salt and freshly ground black pepper

To open the oysters, wrap one hand in a tea towel and hold the oyster in it with the flat shell uppermost. Push the point of an oyster knife into the hinge, located at the narrowest point, and wiggle the knife back and forth until the hinge breaks and you can slide the knife between the two shells. Twist the point of the knife upwards to lever up the top shell, cut through the ligament attaching the oyster to the top shell and lift the shell off. Release the oyster meat from the bottom shell, pick out any little bits of shell and then pour away all the juices. Arrange the oysters in their shells on 4 plates.

Mix together the shallots, tarragon, parsley, mustard, soy sauce, oil, lemon juice, Pernod and a little seasoning to taste in a small bowl. Spoon a little of the sauce onto each oyster and serve straight away.

Bastia, Corsica

I HAVE ALWAYS BEEN of the opinion that most fish is better if a little undercooked, but I'm somewhat revising this now. This is particularly the case with swordfish – it isn't nice if it's too pink. Equally, it's often disappointing in countries like Italy and Greece where it can be cooked until dry. It has to be just right. The ideal temperature in the centre is 55–60°C. I earnestly recommend you buy a probe-type thermometer – they're not expensive. But if you don't have one, there should be the merest blush of pink in the centre of the thickest part of the steak. I tested this recipe with steaks that were 2 cm thick, and when cooked for 4 minutes on each side over a medium-high heat they were perfect. Salmoriglio is practically the only show in town in Sicily where grilled fish steaks are concerned, and frankly it can't be bettered. The combination of lemon juice, peppery olive oil, garlic and oregano is all you need. Tuna would make a good alternative fish but in this case it's imperative to undercook it – about 45°C in the centre is perfect. *Serves 4*

SEARED SWORDFISH STEAKS
WITH SALMORIGLIO
SICILY

4 x 200–225-g swordfish steaks, about 2
  cm thick
A little olive oil
Salt, peperoncino or crushed dried chillies,
  and freshly ground black pepper
For the salmoriglio
6 tablespoons extra virgin olive oil

3 tablespoons water
1½ tablespoons lemon juice
1 garlic clove, very finely chopped
1 tablespoon chopped oregano
1 tablespoon chopped celery herb or
  celery tops (optional)
1 tablespoon chopped flat-leaf parsley

If you are using a charcoal barbecue, light it 40 minutes before you want to start cooking. If you are using a gas barbecue, light it 10 minutes beforehand. If you are using a ridged cast-iron griddle, leave it over a high heat for a couple of minutes until smoking hot, then reduce the heat to medium-high.

Shortly before cooking the swordfish, make the salmoriglio. Whisk the olive oil and water together in a bowl until thick and creamy and then whisk in the lemon juice and some salt to taste. Stir in the garlic, oregano, celery herb, if using, and parsley.

Brush the swordfish generously with olive oil and season well with salt, peperoncino or crushed dried chillies and black pepper. Cook over a medium-high heat for 4 minutes on each side. Serve with the salmoriglio.

AS FAR AS I CAN TELL, this recipe originated in the 1960s when tourism really took off in Corfu. I like the idea of a recipe whose origins are not lost in the mists of time. This has a very 1960s feel about it, and why shouldn't a recipe conjure up a decade just as well as plastic furniture, miniskirts or Dusty Springfield hairdos? It's extremely moreish too. The combination of ouzo, a well-flavoured tomato sauce and some feta served with some, preferably, barbecued prawns (although you can do them under the grill too) is irresistible. *Serves 4 as a starter or 8 as part of a mixed mezze*

GRILLED PRAWNS
WITH OUZO, TOMATOES, CHILLI AND FETA
CORFU

3 tablespoons olive oil

4 garlic cloves, crushed

1 small onion, finely chopped

¼ teaspoon crushed dried chillies

1 x 400-g and 1 x 200-g can chopped
   tomatoes

3 tablespoons ouzo or Pernod, plus extra
   for sprinkling

1 kg large, raw, shell-on prawns

A little olive oil, for brushing

175 g Greek feta cheese, crumbled

A small handful of wild fennel herb,
   roughly chopped

Salt and freshly ground black pepper

Wild fennel herb sprigs, to garnish

Put the olive oil and garlic into a frying pan and place over a medium-high heat. As soon as the garlic begins to sizzle around the edges, add the onion and crushed dried chillies and cook gently until soft but not browned. Add the tomatoes and 2 tablespoons of the ouzo and simmer for 7–10 minutes until thickened slightly. Season well with salt and pepper and keep hot.

You can either barbecue or grill the prawns. If you are using a charcoal barbecue, light it 40 minutes before you want to start cooking. If you are using a gas barbecue or grill, turn it on 10 minutes beforehand.

Peel the prawns, leaving the last tail segment of the shell in place. Put them into a bowl and toss with the remaining ouzo, ½ teaspoon salt and some freshly ground black pepper. Set aside for 5 minutes.

Thread the prawns onto pairs of parallel thin skewers – this will stop them from spinning round when you come to turn them. Brush them lightly with olive oil and barbecue or grill for 1½ minutes on each side until cooked through.

Stir half of the feta cheese into the tomato sauce with the wild fennel herb and spoon it over the base of 1 large or 4 individual warmed serving dishes. Push the prawns off the skewers onto the top of the sauce and sprinkle with the remaining feta. Garnish with the fennel sprigs and serve hot.

JEN JEN WAS a bit of a character. We met him in Ajaccio, where he has a restaurant called Le Bilboquet, and, as far as I could tell, he had only one dish on the menu: local lobster served with pasta. He works on his own and each evening he makes an enormous pan of tomato sauce with fresh lobster to which he adds cognac, herbes de Provence and an ingredient typical in fish cookery in Corsica and France: curry powder. Used as I am to simply grilling fresh lobster, the idea of making this vat of highly expensive lobster in tomato sauce and serving it up over the course of an evening with copious amounts of pasta seemed a bit brutal, but I really enjoyed it. I felt a bit of fellowship with Jen Jen. As well as being an ex-boxer, he also used to run a nightclub locally, like me before I opened my restaurant. Have a disco that is, not be a boxer. Mind you, I was knocked out at least twice while I ran the nightclub in Padstow. Anyway, I got on thoroughly well with Jen Jen. He was obsessed with Napoleon, unusually for a Corsican, and the local but later national heart-throb, singer Tino Rossi. Indeed there are massive paintings in Jen Jen's restaurant of Jen Jen himself, Tino, and a rather stroppy-looking Napoleon, all looking distinctly overfed, presumably after a large serving of lobster with pasta. Canadian lobster, which is less expensive than British, is easy to get hold of in Britain, and fine for this dish. *Serves 2*

LOBSTER
AND PASTA CHEZ JEN JEN
CORSICA

1 x 750-g cooked Canadian lobster
200 g dried spaghetti
100 ml extra virgin olive oil
1 garlic clove, finely chopped
¼ teaspoon curry powder
20 ml Cognac

50 ml dry white wine
200 ml sieved canned tomatoes, such as passata
1 teaspoon dried herbes de Provence
Salt and cayenne pepper

Lay the lobster, belly-side down, on a chopping board and make sure none of the legs are tucked underneath. Cut it in half, first, with the head towards you, cutting through the middle between the eyes, then turn either the knife or the lobster 180°C and finish cutting it in half through the tail. Separate the pieces and remove the dark intestinal tract from the tail meat. Remove the soft green tomalley (liver) and any red roe from the head section and set aside. Pull out the stomach sac and discard. Crack the claws and leg joints with the back of a large sharp knife.

Bring 4.5 litres water to the boil in a large saucepan with 8 teaspoons salt. Add the spaghetti and cook for 9 minutes or until *al dente*.

Put the olive oil, garlic and curry powder into a sauté pan, and as soon as the garlic starts to sizzle, add the lobster, flesh-side down. Pour over the Cognac and set alight to burn off the alcohol. Add the white wine, tomato passata, herbes de Provence and the reserved tomalley and roe, cover and leave to simmer for 5 minutes or until the lobster has heated through.

Drain the spaghetti. Lift the lobster halves onto warmed plates, placing them flesh-side up. Season the sauce to taste with salt and cayenne pepper, add the pasta and toss together well. Spoon alongside the lobster and serve.

THIS SPECIAL DISH from the Rif area of northern Africa gets its name from the shallow, round, unglazed terracotta baking dish in which it is cooked. It's especially popular in the small restaurants that surround the fish market in Tangiers. I noticed two things while I was enjoying a tagra there one lunchtime: first, a procession of youths coming in to sell little plastic bags of sardines they had picked up, which had fallen from the wooden boxes being unloaded manually from the boats in the port. It's a poor country. There were also two boys of about 17 or 18 who were ravenously sharing a tagra on the table next to me. Somebody told us they had been discovered hiding in a lifeboat on one of the ferries leaving Tangiers for Algeciras in Spain, and they had jumped into the harbour water to escape capture. They were planning to crawl under a truck later that night in a second attempt to get to southern Spain and find work. They were nice-looking, desperate young men, not criminals. Unemployment in Morocco is more than 25 per cent. The tagra there was good, but this one from Casa Hassan in Chefchaouen is exceptionally good. *Serves 4*

SARDINE TAGRA

MOROCCO

20 small sardines, butterflied (see page 20)

450g skinned, seeded and chopped tomatoes

1 large onion, very finely chopped

450g medium-sized waxy potatoes, such as Charlotte, peeled and sliced

1 beef tomato, sliced

1 small lemon, thinly sliced

1 small green pepper, sliced

6 small dried red chillies

2 tablespoons olive oil

Juice ½ lemon

A pinch dried oregano

Salt

For the charmoula

4 tablespoons chopped fresh coriander

2 tablespoons crushed garlic

1 teaspoon ground cumin

1½ tablespoons paprika

½ teaspoon freshly ground black pepper

1 teaspoon salt

2 large pinches dried oregano

3 tablespoons olive oil

Preheat the oven to 200°C/Gas Mark 6. Put all the ingredients for the charmoula into a mortar and pound to a paste with the pestle. Sandwich the butterflied sardines together in pairs with some of the charmoula and set them aside on a plate.

Tip the chopped tomatoes into a 26-cm tagra or shallow baking dish, add the onion and the rest of the charmoula and mix together well. Then cover with overlapping slices of the potato, press them down well and season with a little salt. Arrange the sardine 'sandwiches' on top, placing them round the edge of the dish like the spokes of a wheel. Overlap the tomato and lemon slices on top of the sardines, round the edge of the dish, followed by the slices of green pepper. Place one dried red chilli in the centre of each pepper slice, then drizzle over the olive oil and lemon juice, sprinkle with the dried oregano and season with a little more salt.

Bake the tagra for 1–1¼ hours until the potatoes are tender, covering loosely with a sheet of foil towards the end of cooking if it starts to get too brown. Serve straight away with fresh bread.

THIS IS YET ANOTHER recipe inspired by my visit to the Boqueria market in La Rambla in Barcelona. What I particularly like is the way the market radiates out from fish right in the centre, through shellfish, dried and preserved fish, to meat and then vegetables and fruit on the outer edge. Very telling; I felt at the time that fish is the centre of the Catalan universe. This is a celebration of that market: fish, meat and vegetables in one dish. It's the sort of dish that most people I know would put at the top of their list when selecting a first course. Choose a small, thin type of chorizo sausage, rather than those the size of a salami. *Serves 4*

SAUTÉED SQUID
AND CHORIZO SALAD WITH GARLIC, ROCKET, TOMATOES AND CHICKPEAS

CATALONIA

100 g dried chickpeas, soaked overnight

300 g prepared medium-sized squid or cuttlefish

8 cherry tomatoes, quartered

1½ tablespoons lemon juice

6 tablespoons extra virgin olive oil

1 medium-hot red chilli, seeded and thinly sliced across

2 garlic cloves, finely chopped

A small handful of flat-leaf parsley leaves, chopped

50 g chorizo picante (hot chorizo sausage), cut across into thin slices

15–20 g rocket leaves

Salt and coarsely ground black pepper

Drain the soaked chickpeas, put them into a pan and cover with fresh cold water. Bring to the boil and simmer until the skins begin to crack and they are tender – about 40 minutes – adding 1 teaspoon salt to the pan 5 minutes before the end of the cooking time. Drain and leave to cool.

Cut the body pouch of each squid open along one side and score the inner side with the tip of a small, sharp knife into a fine diamond pattern. Then cut each pouch lengthways in half, then across into 7.5-cm pieces.

Stir the tomatoes into the chickpeas with the lemon juice, 4 tablespoons of the olive oil, the chilli, garlic, flat-leaf parsley and some salt and pepper to taste.

Heat 1 tablespoon of the remaining olive oil in a large frying pan over a high heat. Add half the squid pieces, scored side facing upwards first (this will make them curl attractively), and half the tentacles and sear for 30 seconds, then turn them over and sear for another 30 seconds until golden brown and caramelized. Season with salt and pepper and remove from the pan. Repeat with the remaining tablespoon of olive oil and the rest of the squid. Return all the squid to the pan with the chorizo and toss together over a high heat for a further minute.

Briefly toss the rocket leaves through the chickpea salad and spoon onto 1 large or 4 individual plates. Top with the sautéed squid and chorizo and serve.

IN CORFU we thought we'd lined up some really interesting filming of 'jigging' for squid. This is the process by which a large, multi-hooked lure is jerked up and down through the water to catch them. It's common to do this at night using powerful lights, which attract the squid in large quantities. We were in the little fishing port near Melikia in the south of the island, so we talked to the fishermen, and that afternoon, after the fishing boats had set sail, we hired a fast launch from Corfu town to follow them. We travelled for a couple of hours until we were off the island of Paxos, but all we found were two platforms floating in the sea with lights beaming down into the water. Where were the fishermen? We never saw a boat, and to this day I have no idea what went wrong. Sadly, I've still never seen the squid being caught this way. This is the perfect seafood for cooking on the barbecue as the smoky flavour from the coals is so good with it. I've scored the squid into a diamond-shaped pattern that makes it curl attractively, and the skewers are essential to stop the pieces falling through the bars. The warm potatoes, the spring onions and the slightly peppery, red wine vinegar dressing are all you need in addition. *Serves 4*

SKEWERS OF SQUID
COOKED OVER CHARCOAL WITH AN OREGANO AND HOT RED PEPPER DRESSING
CORFU

2 medium-sized squid (about 600 g), cleaned

5 tablespoons extra virgin olive oil, plus extra for brushing

A generous pinch of crushed dried chillies

450 g firm, yellow-fleshed new potatoes, peeled, scrubbed or scraped clean

1½ tablespoons red wine vinegar

1 teaspoon dried oregano

A pinch of Aleppo pepper or cayenne pepper

4 spring onions, trimmed and thinly sliced

Salt and freshly ground black pepper

If you are using a charcoal barbecue, light it 40 minutes before you want to start cooking. If you are using a gas barbecue, light it 10 minutes beforehand.

Cut the body pouch of each squid open along one side and score the inner side with the tip of a small, sharp knife into a fine diamond pattern. Cut each pouch lengthways into 3 strips and then each one across into 3 even-sized pieces. Separate each set of tentacles into pairs. Roll up each piece of squid, scored-side outermost, and thread four pieces of squid and a couple of tentacle pairs onto four 20-cm-long fine metal skewers. Brush with olive oil, season with salt and pepper, and sprinkle with the crushed dried chillies.

Bring a small pan of well-salted water to the boil. Meanwhile, cut the potatoes across into 4–5mm-thick slices. Drop the potato slices into the boiling water and cook for 5 minutes, or until just tender. Drain, return to the pan, cover and keep warm.

For the dressing, whisk together the red wine vinegar and 5 tablespoons olive oil, then stir in the dried oregano, Aleppo or cayenne pepper and ¼ teaspoon salt.

Barbecue the squid skewers for 2 minutes on each side until just cooked through. Overlap the warm potato slices in the centre of four plates, scatter with the spring onions and rest one skewer of squid on top. Spoon over some of the dressing and serve straight away.

IT IS NO EXAGGERATION to say that my enthusiasm for red mullet cooked over charcoal somewhere in Greece was one of the prime motivations for opening a fish restaurant in Padstow in the first place. There's something about its pure simplicity that inspired me to try to treat our Cornish fish with the same respect. I'm always looking for ways to do justice to fish, and I think this, based on the idea of an escabeche, really does accentuate the sweet firmness of the flesh and the nuttiness of the skin of this fish, favoured above all by the Romans. It also looks very pretty with the reds of the chilli and tomato, and the greens of the spring onions and tarragon. *Serves 4 as a starter*

FRIED RED MULLET
WITH A HOT DRESSING OF OLIVE OIL, SPRING ONIONS, GARLIC AND TARRAGON
CORFU

4 red mullet, each weighing about 180–200 g, cleaned and trimmed

2 tablespoons plain flour

8 tablespoons extra virgin olive oil

3 garlic cloves, thinly sliced

2 medium-hot red chillies, seeded and thinly sliced on the diagonal

1 bunch spring onions, trimmed and cut on the diagonal into 3-cm pieces

4 cherry tomatoes, quartered

1 tablespoon tarragon leaves

2 tablespoons red wine vinegar

Salt and freshly ground black pepper

Crusty fresh bread, to serve

Season the fish on both sides with salt and pepper and then dust with the plain flour and knock off the excess.

Heat 2 tablespoons of the olive oil in a large frying pan, add the red mullet and fry over a medium heat for 4 minutes on each side until cooked through. When you part the flesh near the head it should show signs of coming cleanly away from the bones. Remove to a serving plate and keep warm. Pour away any remaining oil and wipe the pan clean.

Add another 2 tablespoons of oil to the pan with the garlic, chilli, spring onions, cherry tomatoes and tarragon leaves and fry for 2–3 minutes over a medium heat. Add the vinegar, let it bubble down to almost nothing, season with salt and pepper and then stir in the remaining olive oil. Pour the mixture evenly over the fish and serve straight away with plenty of fresh bread for mopping up the juices.

I WANTED TO BRING attention to the uniquely firm, fresh flavour of good monkfish so I've accompanied it with a vegetable stew made with the flavours of olive oil, fennel, ouzo and green olives. The stew is cooked until the vegetables are quite soft and the flavours are concentrated, then I thicken it with just a tablespoon of mayonnaise and finish it with a sprinkle of wild fennel herb, which grows all over the island of Corfu. *Serves 4 as a starter*

ROAST MONKFISH
WITH A STEW OF FENNEL, GARLIC AND GREEN OLIVES
CORFU

6 tablespoons extra virgin olive oil

2 fennel bulbs, sliced across into horse-shoes

6 garlic cloves, thinly sliced

80 ml dry white wine

1 tablespoon ouzo or Pernod

150 ml *Chicken stock* (see page 211)

2 x 225-g fillets monkfish, trimmed

2 tablespoons plain flour, seasoned

1 tablespoon *Mayonnaise* (see page 211)

6 green olives, pitted and cut lengthways into thin shards

A handful of wild fennel herb or the frondy tops from the bulbs, roughly chopped

Salt and freshly ground white pepper

Fennel sprigs, to garnish

Preheat the oven to 200°C/Gas Mark 6. Heat 4 tablespoons of the oil in a flameproof casserole measuring about 26 cm across. Add the fennel and garlic and cook gently for about 2 minutes until the fennel begins to soften. Add the white wine, ouzo or Pernod and chicken stock, season with a little salt and pepper, cover and cook over a gentle heat for 10 minutes until quite tender.

Meanwhile, season the monkfish fillets well with salt and pepper and coat them in the seasoned flour. Heat the remaining 2 tablespoons of olive oil in an ovenproof frying pan, add the monkfish and sear for about 3 minutes, turning them 3 or 4 times, until nicely browned on all sides. Transfer the pan to the oven and roast for 6 minutes, until the fish is cooked through but still moist and juicy in the centre.

Remove the fish from the oven, cover with foil and set aside to rest for 5 minutes. Meanwhile, uncover the fennel stew and remove a tablespoon or two of the liquid. Stir it into the mayonnaise, then stir the mixture into the stew and heat very gently to thicken it slightly, but do not let it get too hot or it will curdle. Stir in the green olives and fennel herb or fronds and adjust the seasoning to taste.

Cut the monkfish across, slightly on the diagonal, into thick slices. Spoon some of the fennel stew into the centre of each warmed plate and place the monkfish on top. Garnish with sprigs of fennel and serve.

SEA BREAM

WITH A SAUCE VIERGE OF BABY FENNEL, SPRING ONIONS, TOMATO AND MINT

CORSICA

THIS DISH COMES from a really attractive seafood restaurant, Le Pirate, in the fishing village of Erbalunga, just outside Bastia on Corsica. I sat by the harbour waiting for this marvellous fresh-tasting fish to arrive, admiring a splendid house overlooking the sea in a romantic state of dereliction and reading a book on Corsica by Dorothy Carrington, called *Granite Island*. In it she says: 'Corsican peasant food, if rather repetitive, can be delicious; but the marvel of it is in the quality of the products, all freshly taken from the land and yielding, often, subtle, unexpected flavours in which aroma can hardly distinguish from taste.' Interestingly enough, she doesn't mention food from the sea: traditionally Corsicans settled in the mountains because the coastline was swampy, riddled with malaria and under constant threat of pirates. Thankfully, the pirate threat has receded, and the seafood of this island is superb. *Serves 4 as a starter*

4 heads of baby fennel
1 x 450-g gilt-head bream, cleaned and
trimmed
8 tablespoons extra virgin olive oil, plus extra
for brushing
2 tablespoons lemon juice
4 cherry tomatoes, quartered
2 thin spring onions, trimmed and thinly sliced
2 garlic cloves, thinly sliced
½ medium-hot red chilli, seeded and thinly
sliced across
6 mint leaves, finely shredded
Salt and freshly ground black pepper

Bonifacio, Corsica

Preheat the grill to high. Trim the baby fennel down to 15 cm and then cut each one in half, lengthways. Drop them into a pan of boiling, lightly salted water and blanch for 1½ minutes until *al dente*. Drain and refresh under cold water. Drain well on kitchen pepper.

Brush the fish on both sides with olive oil, season with salt and pepper and place on an oiled baking tray or the rack of the grill pan. Cook for 10 minutes, turning it over halfway through. Meanwhile, put the oil, lemon juice, tomatoes, spring onions, garlic, chilli, ½ teaspoon of salt and 10 turns of the black pepper mill into a small pan. Set aside.

Lift the fish onto a chopping board. Using a small, sharp knife, cut through the skin all around the outside edge of the fish, across the base of the tail and behind the gills, and pull it away. Run your knife down the length of the fish between the two top

fillets, and ease them apart and away from the underlying bones. Slide a palette knife under each of the fillets in turn and carefully lift them away. Set them aside on a warmed plate. Now, lift up the backbone of the fish by the tail and carefully ease it away from the bottom fillets, taking the head with it, and discard. Slice down the centre of the bottom fillets and clean away any bones and skin from the outside edges. Lift the bottom fillets away from the skin and add them to the plate.

Add the pieces of blanched fennel to the pan of sauce vierge and place it over a low heat. Warm through gently for 1 minute. First lift out the fennel and overlap 2 pieces in the centre of each warmed serving plate. Put one fish fillet on top. Stir the mint leaves into the remaining sauce, spoon a little over the fish and fennel and serve straight away.

THE THING THAT most impressed me about this skate dish from Il Caminetto in Cabras was the tomato sauce with sultanas and saffron. I've never tasted anything quite like it. It's so easy to do, and it's something really quite special. They served it at room temperature as an antipasto along with some other dishes but it's equally good served warm, particularly with a good Vermentino, the excellent local white wine. Incidentally, a great one is La Cala; the producers are Sella and Mosca. *Serves 4 as a starter*

BURRIDA ALLA CABRARESE:
SKATE WITH TOMATO, SAFFRON, GARLIC AND SULTANAS
SARDINIA

2 x 225-g skinned and trimmed skate wings

For the tomato, saffron and sultana sauce

100 ml extra virgin olive oil

6 garlic cloves, finely chopped

400-g can good quality plum tomatoes, such as San Marzano

30 g sultanas

A pinch of saffron strands

A pinch of crushed dried chillies

2 fresh bay leaves

1 teaspoon sugar

1 teaspoon small capers, drained and rinsed, to serve

Salt and freshly ground black pepper

For the sauce, put the olive oil and garlic into a medium-sized pan. Place over a medium heat and as soon as the garlic begins to sizzle, add the tomatoes, sultanas, saffron, dried chillies, bay leaves, sugar and ½ teaspoon salt. Bring up to a gentle simmer and leave to cook for 30 minutes, stirring every now and then, and breaking up the tomatoes with a wooden spoon. Remove the bay leaves, season to taste with salt and pepper and keep warm.

Bring 1.5 litres water to the boil in a large shallow pan. Add 1 tablespoon salt and the skate wings and leave them to simmer gently for 10 minutes until cooked.

Lift the skate wings out of the water onto a board and cut each one into 2 or 3 pieces. Spoon slightly more than half the tomato sauce onto the base of a warmed oval serving dish and place the pieces of skate on top. Spoon the rest of the sauce down the centre of the skate, scatter with the capers and serve.

ON MANY OCCASIONS during my journey through the Mediterranean, I found dishes that were memorable eaten at a table by the sea, shaded from the midday sun, but slightly less appealing on paper back in Cornwall. Maybe it's the same as a glass of retsina tasting a whole lot better in Corfu than it does back home. But all I can say is I've tried this dish at home with our own grey mullet and it's lovely. Who would have thought that frying garlic and onions in olive oil, adding potato, grouper (as it was in Corfu) or mullet, oregano and bay leaves and letting everything stew together for 20 minutes or so would result in something so delicious? This dish has Italian roots, and it's called 'white' because it is made without tomatoes. *Serves 4*

BIANCO:

GREY MULLET BRAISED WITH POTATOES, GARLIC, OLIVE OIL AND LEMON JUICE

CORFU

100 ml extra virgin olive oil

2 medium onions, halved and thinly sliced

10 garlic cloves, thinly sliced

1 kg waxy maincrop potatoes, such as Desiree or Charlotte, peeled and cut into 4-cm chunks

1 fresh bay leaf

1 teaspoon chopped fresh oregano

1 x 1.5-kg grey mullet, cleaned and trimmed

Juice ½ small lemon

2 tablespoons chopped flat-leaf parsley

Salt and freshly ground black pepper

Heat 5 tablespoons of the oil in a flameproof casserole about 26 cm across. Add the onions and garlic and cook over a medium heat, stirring, for about 6–7 minutes until soft but not browned. Add the potatoes, season with salt and pepper and cook, stirring gently, until the potatoes are about half done – about 10 minutes. Stir in the bay leaf and oregano.

Cut the grey mullet across into 4-cm-thick steaks, discarding the head and the tail. Place the fish steaks on top of the potatoes, drizzle with the remaining oil and 500 ml water. Season with salt and pepper. Part-cover the casserole and simmer over a medium heat for 20–25 minutes until the fish is cooked through and flaky and the liquid has reduced slightly.

Adjust the seasoning, sprinkle over the lemon juice, garnish with the chopped parsley and serve.

I WATCHED THIS being made in a small Sardinian restaurant and was struck by the tiny amount of cuttlefish ink – little more than a teaspoon – that will turn about 300 ml of tomato sauce jet black. Don't be put off by the idea that the ink will give the pasta dish a murky flavour. What you will have is a good tomato-sauced pasta that just looks black from the ink and has a slight scent of seafood in the background. And it feels so jolly to be eating it – a bit like Heston Blumenthal's food but from a fisherman's café in Portixeddu. *Serves 4*

SPAGHETTI AL NERO DE SEPIA:
SPAGHETTI WITH TOMATO, GARLIC AND CUTTLEFISH INK
SARDINIA

1-kg whole cuttlefish

400 g dried spaghetti

4 tablespoons extra virgin olive oil

1 small onion, chopped

¼ teaspoon peperoncino or crushed dried chillies

2 garlic cloves, finely chopped

300 ml *Tomato sauce* (see page 211)

A handful of flat-leaf parsley leaves, chopped

Salt and freshly ground black pepper

To prepare the cuttlefish, cut off the tentacles just in front of the eyes. Remove the beak-like mouth from the centre of the tentacles and throw it away, then pull the skin off the tentacles and set to one side. Cut the head section from the body and discard. Cut open the body section from the top to bottom along the dark-coloured back and remove the cuttle bone and the entrails, carefully removing and reserving one of the ink pouches: a small pearly-white sac in among the entrails. Wash the body well and then pull off the dark skin.

Cut the cuttlefish pouches in half lengthways. If your cuttlefish are quite large, the flesh of the pouch will be quite thick, so cut it across into slices 5–7 mm thick. With smaller cuttlefish, the flesh will be thinner, more like squid. Cut this across into strips 1–1.5 cm wide.

Bring 4.5 litres water to the boil in a large saucepan with 8 teaspoons salt. Add the pasta and cook for 9 minutes or until *al dente*.

Meanwhile, heat the olive oil in a large, deep frying pan, add the onion and peperoncino or crushed dried chillies and fry until soft and lightly golden. Add the garlic and cook for 2 minutes more. Add the prepared cuttlefish and sauté for 3 minutes until lightly golden. Add the tomato sauce and the ink bag, breaking it up in the sauce with a wooden spoon to release the ink. Cook for 2–3 minutes. Season to taste with salt and pepper.

Lift the spaghetti out of the water (a little water will still be clinging to the pasta and will help to loosen the sauce slightly), drop it straight into the cuttlefish sauce and mix together well. Divide between warmed bowls and scatter with a generous amount of chopped parsley before serving.

THOUGH *ZUPPA* translates as 'soup', it usually refers to a dish that contains rather more solids than liquid. I came across this one in a little fishing village called Portixeddu. The restaurant was called L'Ancora and it looked just about OK from the outside. But whereas in Britain if you go into a very ordinary-looking place all you'll get is maybe a cup of tea and some baked beans and chips, in Sardinia you can end up with some great food like cuttlefish with pasta (see my recipe on page 101), grilled sea bass, a bottle of Vermentino, a *zuppa* of shellfish and a passionate cook. *Serves 4*

ZUPPA DI COZZE E ARSELLE:
A STEW OF MUSSELS AND CLAMS SCATTERED OVER CHARGRILLED BREAD
SARDINIA

3 tablespoons extra virgin olive oil, plus extra for drizzling

5 fat garlic cloves, 4 finely chopped and one left whole

A pinch of peperoncino or crushed dried chillies

400-g can chopped tomatoes

3 tablespoons red wine vinegar

2 teaspoons caster sugar

500 g mussels, cleaned

500 g clams, washed

50 ml dry white wine

4 large slices rustic white bread, taken from a large round loaf

2 tablespoons chopped flat-leaf parsley

Put the olive oil, chopped garlic and peperoncino into a large flameproof casserole and place it over a medium heat. As soon as it begins to sizzle, add the tomatoes and 150 ml water and leave to simmer gently for 10 minutes until reduced and thickened. Meanwhile, put the vinegar and sugar into a small pan and boil until reduced to 1 teaspoon. Stir into the tomato sauce and keep hot.

Place another large pan over a high heat and when hot, add the mussels, clams and white wine, cover and cook for 2–3 minutes until the shellfish have just opened. Tip the mussels, clams and all but the last tablespoon or two of the cooking juices (which might be a bit gritty) into the tomato sauce and stir together well.

Toast the slices of bread on both sides and then singe over a naked gas flame for a slightly smoky taste. Rub one side of each slice of toast with the peeled garlic clove, put the slices of toast into the base of 4 warmed bistro-style plates and drizzle with a little olive oil. Stir the parsley into the stew, spoon the stew on top of the bread and serve straight away.

Santa Teresa Gallura, Sardinia

I HAVE OFTEN BEEN TOLD by locals in Italy that oily fish and raw onions go very well together, and indeed if you think of the Dutch passion for matjes (herring and onion), for example, you begin to see there is a natural affinity and that appreciation for it is quite widespread. During a trip to Japan I came across a similar harmony between oily fish and hot radish, or daikon as it's known. All of which helps explain the considerable success of this popular way with fish in Sicily. The fish I first tried it with was sabre fish, but I found gurnard, which is nothing like as oily as herring or mackerel but is still quite rich, is superb dusted with seasoned flour, fried in olive oil and then served with these sweet and sour onions. The secret with the accompaniment is to cook the onions only long enough that they still have a subtle *al dente* bite, and to use red wine vinegar, and honey instead of sugar for the sweetness. *Serves 4*

FRIED GURNARD
WITH SWEET AND SOUR RED ONIONS
SICILY

Olive oil, for shallow frying
8 x 75-g fillets of gurnard
50 g plain flour
1 teaspoon small capers, to garnish
Salt and freshly ground black pepper

For the sweet and sour onions
50 ml extra virgin olive oil
2 medium red onions, halved and thinly sliced
2 tablespoons red wine vinegar
2 tablespoons clear honey

For the sweet and sour onions, heat the olive oil in a frying pan. Add the onions, vinegar, honey, ½ teaspoon salt and some pepper and cook them gently for 10 minutes, stirring every now and then, until they are soft but still with a little bite, but do not let them brown. Keep warm.

Pour the olive oil into a wide shallow pan to a depth of 1 cm and heat it to 180°C. Season the fish fillets on both sides with salt and pepper and then coat them in the plain flour and knock off the excess. Lower the heat slightly under the pan, add the fish fillets and cook them for 1 minute on each side until lightly golden and cooked through. Lift onto kitchen paper and drain briefly.

Overlap 2 fish fillets in the centre of each warmed plate and spoon over some of the sweet and sour onions. Scatter with the capers and serve. Or arrange in pairs on a single serving dish before spooning over the onions and capers.

THE ORIGINAL RECIPE FOR BOTTARGA with pasta came from Sardinia, which I think is where the best bottarga comes from, and the recipe was simply pasta with olive oil, garlic, a pinch of chilli, parsley and bottarga, with as far as I can remember a squeeze of lemon juice. It was memorable, but you've really got to like your bottarga. In case you've forgotten, bottarga is the salted roe of the grey mullet. To me it's as heavenly as caviar but I think for most people a little goes a long way, and just as well as it's very expensive too. So I've devised a recipe bringing in prawns and spring onions, where the bottarga is grated over the finished pasta much like parmesan. I love it, but be warned: don't drink a fine wine with it because it makes the wine taste bitter. I suggest a Vermentino from Sardinia, but not your best. *Serves 4*

LINGUINE WITH BOTTARGA,
PRAWNS, CHILLI AND SPRING ONIONS
SARDINIA

400 g dried linguine

3 tablespoons extra virgin olive oil, plus extra to serve

2 garlic cloves, finely chopped

¼ teaspoon crushed dried chillies

300 g raw headless prawns, peeled

1 bunch spring onions, trimmed and thinly sliced

A small handful of flat-leaf parsley leaves, chopped

4 lemon wedges

15 g bottarga

Salt and freshly ground black pepper

Bring 4.5 litres water to the boil in a large saucepan with 8 teaspoons salt. Add the pasta and cook for 7–8 minutes or until *al dente*.

Just before the pasta is ready, heat the oil in a frying pan. Add the garlic and cook gently over a medium heat for 30 seconds. Add the crushed dried chillies, prawns and some seasoning and leave to sizzle for a few seconds until the prawns turn pink and are just cooked through. Add the spring onions and cook for another 30 seconds until they have slightly softened. Set aside.

Drain the pasta, return it to the pan, add the prawn and spring onion mixture and the parsley and toss together well.

Divide the pasta between 4 warmed pasta plates and drizzle with a little more oil. Squeeze over a few drops of lemon juice and then finely grate over the bottarga, just like you would parmesan. Serve immediately.

THE HAKE FISHING in the bay of St George is particularly good due to the large number of sunken British ships, torpedoed there in the First World War. I had an exhilarating early morning's fishing there about 12 miles out of L'Ametlla de Mar. We brought the fish back to the Café Xavier and filmed a passionate chef called Rosa cooking this simple but lovely hake dish. She pounded garlic, tomato, parsley and olive oil together in a mortar and used this to braise the fish, along with a little water. On my odyssey of the Mediterranean I was constantly amazed by the intense flavour of just a few ingredients. I ate this with great gusto, with some fresh bread and a glass of Albariño. *Serves 4*

SUQUET DE PEIX:
HAKE BRAISED WITH POUNDED GARLIC, PARSLEY, TOMATO AND PIMENTÓN
CATALONIA

1 x 175-g ripe beef tomato, skinned, seeded and roughly chopped

A large handful of flat-leaf parsley leaves, roughly chopped

6 garlic cloves, sliced

1 teaspoon pimentón picante (hot paprika)

100 ml extra virgin olive oil

4 x 150-g pieces of thick hake fillet, taken from a medium-size fish

25 g plain flour

100 ml hot water

1 teaspoon lemon juice

Salt

Crusty fresh bread, to serve

Put the tomato, parsley and garlic into a mortar or mini food processor and pound or blend until smooth. Add the pimentón.

Heat the olive oil in a large, deep frying pan, add the pounded mixture and fry for 3–4 minutes until you can smell the garlic starting to colour. Add 300 ml cold water and leave it to simmer until reduced by half.

Season the pieces of hake with salt and then dust with the flour, knocking off the excess. Add the hake to the pan, spoon some of the sauce over each piece, cover and cook, shaking the pan gently once or twice to prevent the fish sticking, for 5 minutes until just done.

Lift the fish onto warmed plates, and add the hot water and lemon juice to the remaining sauce. Simmer briefly, stirring, until the oil becomes amalgamated into the sauce once more. Season to taste with salt, spoon over the fish and serve with crusty fresh bread.

THE SICILIANS make carpaccio with both tuna and swordfish. They are particularly fond of lightly smoked swordfish presented like this, although I tend to think salmon is a much better fish for smoking. But they do have excellent tuna. We stayed in a converted *tonnara* (tuna factory) called Tonnara di Bonagia just outside Trapani, and I remember doing a slightly sad talk to the camera about the decline of fishing generally, as I sat on one of a row of derelict tuna fishing boats. But nevertheless, if you can find tuna from a good, sustainable source, this is a lovely dish, and very *à la mode* in Italy at the moment, where raw fish dishes are simply called *crudo*. *Serves 4*

TUNA CARPACCIO
WITH A MUSTARD DRESSING, CAPERS, TOMATO AND MINT
SICILY

225-g piece of tuna loin fillet, taken from towards the tail end so it measures about 10 cm across

1 ripe vine tomato, skinned, seeded and cut into small neat dice

1 teaspoon small capers, drained and rinsed

4 mint leaves, very finely shredded

4 flat-leaf parsley leaves, very finely shredded

Sea salt flakes

Freshly ground black pepper

For the mustard dressing

1 teaspoon Dijon mustard

1 teaspoon white wine vinegar

2 tablespoons extra virgin olive oil

Trim the piece of tuna to remove any blood-red flesh and sinews and to give it a nice shape. Then wrap it tightly in some clingfilm and place it in the freezer for about 3 hours until it is firm but not completely frozen.

Remove the tuna from the freezer, unwrap and place on a chopping board. Cut it across into very thin slices using a very sharp, long-bladed knife.

Arrange about 4 slices of the tuna in a single layer over the base of 4 cold plates, pressing them out slightly so that they butt up together.

For the mustard dressing, whisk the mustard and vinegar together in a small bowl then whisk in the oil 1 teaspoon at a time so that it forms a thick, well-emulsified dressing. Whisk in a few drops of warm water to loosen it slightly and season to taste with some salt and pepper.

Using a teaspoon, drizzle the mustard dressing over the tuna in a zigzag fashion. Then scatter some of the diced tomato, capers, shredded mint and parsley over each plate. Sprinkle with some sea salt flakes and black pepper and serve straight away.

FREE-RANGE
CHICKENS
AND EGGS

YOU ALWAYS FIND CHICKENS
AND EGGS IN THE MEDITERRANEAN
THAT TASTE FABULOUS

Valldemossa, Mallorca

I HAVE BEEN THE VICTIM of many bad paellas in my life, and I sometimes wonder if it isn't all just hype. It's the same with other world-famous dishes – bouillabaisse and cassoulet are two more perfect examples. When they are good they are very, very good, but when they are bad they are horrid. I think there are two main concerns with paellas. First, the rice must be proper paella rice – arroz calasparra – and second, it shouldn't contain too much long-cooked seafood, which ends up tasting like stewed tea. It's also important that once the rice is added to the pan, it is not touched. In paella, you are trying to produce the exact opposite to risotto. In other words, all the grains of rice should be separate (whereas in risotto, by constant stirring, you make it creamy). For my paella I've chosen a mix of chicken, seafood and vegetables. I particularly like the artichoke hearts, and the flavour of rosemary and saffron too, and above all a brilliant stock to start with. Finally, you really do need to get, if not a paella pan, a very large frying pan for this, and if you are cooking this over anything other than a special paella gas burner, then you need to place it over two or even three burners and keep turning the pan so that it cooks evenly through-out. Mind you, true paella pans and burners are easily available over the internet. This is a great dish for a big group of people. *Serves 10–12*

CHICKEN AND PRAWN PAELLA
WITH ARTICHOKES AND CHORIZO
CATALONIA

1 x 1.5-kg chicken

1.75 litres *Chicken stock* (see page 211)

½ teaspoon loosely packed saffron strands

150 ml olive oil

8 garlic cloves, sliced

16 large raw prawns, heads removed but left unpeeled

150 g chorizo picante, sliced

2 medium onions, chopped

2 beef tomatoes, skinned and chopped

750 g arroz calasparra

300 g prepared artichoke hearts (or about 4 medium globe artichokes; see page 209 for preparation)

Leaves from 10-cm rosemary sprig

150 g fine green beans, stalk ends trimmed, cut into 1.5-cm pieces

150 g shelled fresh peas

Salt

Joint the chicken and remove the bones from the breasts and thighs. Cut the knuckle end off each drumstick and leave the wings as they are. Cut the breast and thigh meat into large chunks. You could ask your butcher to do this for you.

Put the stock into a large pan, add the chicken bones and leave to simmer for 20 minutes. Strain into a clean pan, add the saffron strands and keep hot.

Heat 4 tablespoons of the oil in a 40-cm paella pan over a medium-high heat, add the chicken and fry until golden brown. Remove the chicken and set aside on a plate.

Add another 2 tablespoons oil to the pan with half the garlic, the prawns and chorizo sausage, and fry for 1 minute until lightly golden. Set aside on another plate.

Add the onions, the remaining oil (4 tablespoons) and garlic to the pan and cook for 5 minutes until lightly golden. Add the tomatoes and leave to cook over a low heat for 15 minutes until you have a jam-like consistency.

Add the rice to the pan, turn up the heat and fry for a minute or two. Then add the stock, the chicken pieces, the artichokes, rosemary and 2 teaspoons of salt and stir briefly to distribute everything evenly around the pan. Leave to simmer for 20 minutes, turning the pan now and then if necessary so that it cooks evenly.

Meanwhile, drop the beans into a pan of boiling salted water and cook for 3 minutes. Drain and refresh under cold water.

Scatter the beans, peas, prawns and chorizo over the top of the rice and cook for a further 10 minutes, by which time the rice should have absorbed all the stock and be tender, and all the other ingredients should be cooked. A slightly brown crust on the base of the paella is acceptable but take care not to let it burn during cooking.

Leave the paella to rest off the heat for 5 minutes before serving. The Spanish prefer to serve it warm rather than hot.

THIS IS ONE of the rare occasions where I am using a hard-to-get ingredient: in this case, sobrasada. This is a soft and spreadable Mallorcan sausage made with pork loin and fat, paprika, salt and varying amounts of cayenne pepper. Some versions are mild, some hot and spicy. Its unique quality, apart from its flavour, is that it melts on cooking; it's used more like a condiment than a sausage. Anyone who has been to Mallorca will know it and probably love it, but as far as I know it's impossible to get in the UK at present, though I hope to stock it in my deli. As an alternative, use slices of chorizo picante. I serve this with either steamed rice or cooked pasta, or even just fresh crusty bread. *Serves 4*

CHICKEN WITH SOBRASADA,
COURGETTES AND BUTTER BEANS
MALLORCA

100 g dried butter beans, ideally Judión, soaked overnight, or 225 g butter beans from a jar, drained and rinsed

300 ml *Tomato sauce* (see page 211)

4 free-range chicken breasts

2 tablespoons olive oil

A good pinch of peperoncino or crushed dried chillies

75 g sobrasada, thinly sliced

350 g courgettes, trimmed and cut on the diagonal into slices

A small handful of flat-leaf parsley leaves, chopped

Salt and freshly ground black pepper

If using soaked dried beans, drain them, tip them into a pan and cover with fresh cold water. Bring to the boil and simmer gently for about 20–25 minutes until almost tender. Add ½ teaspoon salt and continue to cook until tender – another 5 minutes. Drain and set aside.

If you haven't already done so, make the tomato sauce according to the instructions on page 211. Set to one side.

Season the chicken breasts on both sides with some salt and pepper. Heat the olive oil in a large frying pan, add the chicken breasts, skin-side down, and cook for 5 minutes over a medium heat until golden brown. Turn over and cook for a further 5 minutes. Move the chicken breasts to one side of the pan and add the peperoncino or chilli flakes and sobrasada, and allow the sobrasada to melt into the oil. Turn the chicken breasts over in the now spicy oil until well coated then lower the heat, scatter over the courgettes, cover and leave to simmer gently for 15 minutes.

Uncover the pan, add the cooked or jarred butter beans and tomato sauce, re-cover and simmer for a further 5 minutes until the beans are heated through. Scatter with the chopped parsley and serve.

THIS IS ONE of the best known dishes of Morocco. It is gloriously different from anything from the other side of the Mediterranean, largely due to the absence of tomatoes, and the presence of preserved lemons, olives and spices such as cinnamon, ginger, saffron and turmeric. The best one I had was in Chefchaouen, at Casa Hassan. Elsewhere they were not nearly so good. I have heard that a lot of Moroccan 'tagine' cookery is actually done in a pressure cooker then transferred to the clay tagine for the tourists' benefit, and quite often this most delicate of tagines then comes out thin and watery. Moroccans traditionally serve this with bread alone, but I really like to serve it with steamed couscous. *Serves 4*

MOROCCAN CHICKEN
WITH PRESERVED LEMON AND OLIVES
MOROCCO

1 x 1.5-kg free-range chicken, with its liver, if possible
1 large onion, finely chopped in a food processor
4 garlic cloves, crushed
100 g butter
1 tbsp ground ginger
7.5-cm piece cinnamon stick
¾ teaspoon turmeric powder

¾ teaspoon saffron strands
Juice 1 lemon (about 3 tablespoons)
100 g green, reddish-brown Moroccan or black Greek kalamata olives
100 g small *Preserved lemons* (see page 209), halved, flesh discarded
10 g coriander leaves, chopped
10 g flat-leaf parsley leaves, chopped
Salt and freshly ground white pepper

Remove the liver and any excess fat from the cavity of the chicken. Discard the fat, cut the liver into small pieces and set it aside in the fridge.

Put the chicken into a flameproof casserole, tagine or saucepan in which it will fit snugly. Add the onion, garlic, butter, ginger, cinnamon stick, turmeric, saffron, 1 teaspoon of salt and some white pepper.

Pour in 700 ml water, cover and bring to the boil over a medium-high heat. Reduce the heat and leave to simmer, spooning the sauce over the chicken and turning it over now and then until it is just cooked through – about 40 minutes.

Lift the chicken onto a plate and cover with foil. Add the lemon juice to the casserole, increase the heat once more and simmer the sauce rapidly until reduced by about two-thirds.

Return the chicken to the casserole with the olives and pieces of preserved lemon, cover with a well-fitting lid and simmer for a further 20–25 minutes until the chicken is tender.

Lift the chicken onto a large warmed oval platter. Add the chicken liver to the sauce and simmer for 5 minutes. Add the herbs and adjust the seasoning if necessary. Spoon the sauce over and around the chicken and serve.

THE CHICKEN IN THIS DISH is spatchcocked: split open down the backbone and flattened out. The Italians call the resulting shape *alla diavola*, 'like the devil', as the shape is said to resemble the devil's face, the legs being his horns. Once the chicken is sprinkled with black pepper and chilli and cooked over a barbecue until a deep reddish-brown and fiery hot, it is delicious. We all want the ultimate crisp and aromatic skin on a barbecued chicken, and this is it. Spatchcock chickens are quite demanding to cook because the legs are thinner than the breast, so you need to move it around from time to time to regulate the cooking. As with the veal chops on page 50, if you have a three-burner gas barbecue, after the initial browning of the surface of the chicken, turn off the middle burner and continue the process by indirect cooking. It's quite simple to do this with a charcoal barbecue too, by pushing the hot coals to the sides. When the chicken is ready, test it with a meat thermometer if you can – it should register 57–60°C in the centre of the breast. Serve green salad and chips alongside – really, nothing beats it. *Serves 4*

POLLO ALLA DIAVOLA:
DEVILLED GRILLED CHICKEN
PUGLIA

1 x 1.5-kg free-range chicken
1 tablespoon black peppercorns
1 teaspoon crushed dried chillies
175 ml olive oil

Juice ½ lemon
2 garlic cloves, crushed
Sea salt
Lemon wedges, to serve

To spatchcock the chicken, put it onto a chopping board, breast-side down, and cut along either side of the backbone with kitchen scissors. Open up the chicken, turn it over and press firmly along the breastbone until it is lying flat.

Coarsely crush the black peppercorns in a mortar using a pestle. Add the chilli flakes and crush a little more, but not too finely.

For the marinade, mix the olive oil with the lemon juice, garlic and ½ teaspoon of salt. Place the chicken in a shallow dish, pour over half the marinade (set the other half aside), and turn it once or twice to make sure it is well coated. Turn it skin-side up and sprinkle with three-quarters of the pepper and chilli mixture. Cover with clingfilm and leave to marinate for at least 1 hour.

If you are using a charcoal barbecue, light it 40 minutes before you want to start cooking and then rearrange the coals for indirect cooking. If using a gas barbecue, light it 10 minutes beforehand, then turn off the middle burners. (See the introduction.) Or you can use the grill, preheated to medium-high.

Mix the remaining black pepper and chilli mixture into the reserved marinade, to use for basting. Remove the chicken from its marinade and season it on both sides with sea salt. Discard the marinade left in the dish.

Place the chicken on the barbecue, carcass-side down and skin-side up, and cook for 15–20 minutes, basting it with a little of the pepper and chilli mixture from time to time. Turn the chicken over and cook for another 15–20 minutes, moving it about and basting it now and then, until it is cooked through and the skin is crispy. If using the grill, cook it on a baking tray, starting it off skin-side down instead.

Lift the chicken onto a board and cut it into pieces. Quickly heat through the remaining pepper and chilli basting mixture, then pour off the excess oil from the surface. Serve the chicken hot with a little of the basting mixture and the lemon wedges.

CHEFCHAOUEN IS A TOWN of surreal blue. It's about a 45-minute drive from the Mediterranean coast and is an absolute must if you're in Tangiers for a few days. This is a simple dish of onions, tomatoes, cumin and paprika baked with spicy little meatballs and eggs. Sometimes, when I visit somewhere particularly special, I think about how much people that I love would love it, and the colour and bustle of Chefchaouen would be absolutely fascinating to my Australian partner, Sarah, but even more so to her young children Zach and Olivia. Olivia is rather fond of eggs, as is her brother, but some days she tells me, 'It's not an egg day.' I think every day would be an egg day in Chefchaouen. You can also do a lovely variation of this dish using sautéed peeled raw prawns instead of meatballs, stirred into the sauce and briefly baked without the eggs. Whichever version you make, serve with warm flatbread. *Serves 4*

KEFTA MKAOUARA:
SPICY EGG, MEATBALL AND TOMATO TAGINE
MOROCCO

3 tablespoons olive oil

4 very fresh medium-sized free-range eggs

A small handful fresh coriander leaves, coarsely chopped, to garnish

Salt and freshly ground black pepper

For the meatballs

450 g minced beef or lamb

2 tablespoons finely chopped parsley

1 teaspoon ground cumin

½ teaspoon hot paprika

For the sauce

1 medium onion, finely chopped

900 g ripe tomatoes, skinned, seeded and chopped or 2 x 400-g cans chopped tomatoes

1 teaspoon ground cumin

½ teaspoon hot paprika

1 teaspoon freshly ground black pepper

2 garlic cloves, crushed

Preheat the oven to 200°C/Gas Mark 6. For the meatballs, put the minced beef, parsley, cumin, paprika, 1 teaspoon salt and some freshly ground black pepper into a bowl and mix together well using your hands. Dampen your hands and form the mixture into about 28 2.5-cm balls.

Heat 2 tablespoons of the oil in a shallow tagine or frying pan and brown the meatballs briefly on all sides. Remove with a slotted spoon to a plate and set to one side.

Add the onion for the sauce to the pan with the remaining tablespoon of oil and cook gently for 10 minutes until very soft and just beginning to brown. Add the remaining sauce ingredients and leave to simmer gently for 15–20 minutes until well concentrated in flavour but not too thick. Season well with salt to taste.

Return the meatballs to the sauce and mix together. Transfer to a shallow ovenproof dish if you have prepared the sauce in a frying pan, otherwise leave the mixture in the tagine. Make 4 slight dips in the mixture and break an egg into each one. Bake in the oven for 15 minutes or until the eggs are just set. Scatter with the chopped coriander and serve.

THIS IS THE SORT of food I love in Greece, what Debbie Major, who works with me, calls 'a rustic, throw-it-together dish'. The more I watched cooks there, the more I was filled with an obvious thought: that cooking shouldn't be difficult. They seem to cook just like breathing. Thrown-together such dishes may appear, but their ingredients are always perfectly balanced. This is a sweet and aromatic mix of sun-dried tomato, onion, oregano, cinnamon and chillies; best served with the rice-shaped pasta known to us by its Italian name, orzo. *Serves 4*

POT-ROASTED CHICKEN
WITH SUN-DRIED TOMATOES, CINNAMON AND OREGANO
CORFU

1 x 2-kg free-range chicken
4 tablespoons extra virgin olive oil
1 large onion, halved and thinly sliced
4 garlic cloves, thinly sliced
60 g sun-dried tomatoes in olive oil, drained
500 g vine-ripened tomatoes, roughly chopped, or 400-g can chopped tomatoes
7.5-cm piece cinnamon stick
1 teaspoon dried oregano

A generous pinch of crushed dried chillies
150 ml *Chicken stock* (see page 211)
400 g orzo or other rice-shaped pasta (see page 207)
25 g butter
50 g finely grated Greek kefalotiri cheese or parmesan cheese
A small handful of flat-leaf parsley leaves, roughly chopped
Salt and freshly ground black pepper

Preheat the oven to 180°C/Gas Mark 4. Season the inside of the chicken. Heat 3 tablespoons of the olive oil in a large flameproof casserole, add the chicken and brown it on all sides over a medium heat. Remove the chicken to a plate, add the remaining oil and the onion to the casserole and cook until soft and lightly browned. Add the garlic, sun-dried tomatoes, fresh or canned tomatoes, cinnamon, oregano, dried chilli flakes, chicken stock, 1 teaspoon of salt and some freshly ground black pepper. Bring to a simmer, replace the chicken and cover the casserole with some foil and a tight-fitting lid.

Transfer the casserole to the oven and bake for 1½ hours until the chicken is very tender.

Shortly before the chicken is ready, bring 4.5 litres water to the boil in a large saucepan with 8 teaspoons

salt. When the chicken is cooked, and the juices from the thickest part of the thigh run clear, lift it onto a carving board, cover it tightly with foil and leave it to rest somewhere warm for 10 minutes. Skim the excess fat from the surface of the sauce, place the casserole over a medium heat and leave to simmer vigorously until the sauce is slightly reduced and thickened.

Meanwhile, drop the orzo into the boiling water and cook for 7 minutes or until *al dente*. Drain and return to the pan with the butter and grated cheese and toss together well.

Remove the cinnamon stick from the sauce, stir in the parsley and adjust the seasoning to taste. Carve the chicken. Spoon some of the sauce onto 4 warmed plates and place the chicken on top. Spoon the orzo alongside and serve.

I DEVISED THIS SALAD using some of the flavours of Morocco as something you might make for a summer lunch party. You can easily double the quantities for a larger group. Dress the salad at the last minute while it's still warm and serve it straight away with chilled Sauvignon-Semillon. This is the type of dish you would get at a party on nice warm summer's evenings in Sydney, where you can buy take-away hot spit-roasted chickens anywhere; replace the chicken in the recipe here with two small, spit-roasted ones, and the dish is very quickly put together. *Serves 6*

WARM ROAST CHICKEN SALAD
WITH BROAD BEANS, BUTTER BEANS, ROCKET AND PRESERVED LEMON
MOROCCO

1 x 1.75-kg free-range chicken
1 red onion, sliced
1 carrot, sliced
1 celery stick, sliced
3 garlic cloves, sliced
Olive oil
Sea salt and freshly ground
   black pepper

For the salad
300 g fresh or frozen shelled
   broad beans

600 g cooked or jarred butter
   beans, ideally Judión, rinsed
   and drained
3 x 25-g pieces *Preserved lemon*
   (see page 209), flesh discarded and rind chopped
2 small red onions, halved and
   thinly sliced
90 g wild rocket
20 g fresh coriander, chopped
20 g fresh mint, leaves chopped

For the dressing
8 tablespoons extra virgin olive
   oil
4 teaspoons lemon juice
½ teaspoon ground cumin
½ teaspoon paprika
A large pinch of cayenne
   pepper
3 small garlic cloves, finely
   chopped

Preheat the oven to 200°C/Gas Mark 6. Rub the chicken all over with olive oil and season well with salt and pepper. Spread the onion, carrot, celery and garlic over the base of a small roasting tin. Place the chicken on top and roast it for 1 hour 40 minutes, or until it is cooked through and the skin is nicely browned.

Remove the chicken from the oven, tipping any juices from the cavity back into the roasting tin, and place it on a board. Cover it loosely with foil and leave it to rest for 15 minutes. Meanwhile, bring a pan of salted water to the boil.

For the dressing, pour the roasting juices from the tin into a sieve set over a small bowl, and press out as much flavour as you can from the vegetables. Skim off and discard the excess oil from the surface of the juices and whisk in the olive oil, lemon juice, cumin, paprika, cayenne and garlic. Season to taste with salt and adjust the balance of lemon juice if necessary.

As soon as the chicken is just cool enough to handle, remove the meat, break it into small chunky pieces and place in a large bowl. Discard the skin and bones. Drop the broad beans into the boiling water and cook for 1–2 minutes until just tender. Add the butter beans, leave for a few seconds to warm through, then drain and add to the chicken with the preserved lemon, red onion, rocket, coriander and mint. Mix together gently using your hands and transfer to a shallow serving dish. Drizzle over the dressing and serve straight away while the salad is still warm.

EVERYWHERE YOU GO IN TURKEY they cook meats over a shallow, trough-shaped charcoal barbecue called a *mangal*. They rarely use gas, favouring charcoal for its dry heat and unique flavour. It is somewhat similar to cooking in a tandoori oven in that the meat doesn't come into contact with anything other than hot, dry, charcoal-scented air, and so doesn't burn on touching hot bars as it can with conventional barbecuing. Unfortunately, therefore, if you want to cook this, or the quail on page 148, you really need to buy a small charcoal brazier – mine cost £23 from Divertimenti in the Brompton Road in West London (they do mail order) – or you'll have to devise some way of removing the grilling rack on your barbecue so you can suspend the skewers of quail over the hot coals. There is no point in cooking these dishes any other way, because they won't taste like they are supposed to. I also wanted to imbue the chicken with some of the common flavours of Turkey, in this case cumin, cinnamon and hot red (Aleppo) pepper. In my opinion, the best way of bringing spicy flavour into barbecued meats is to use yogurt and lemon juice. First you marinate with lemon juice, red pepper and salt, and then you add a second marinade of yogurt, garlic, cumin and cinnamon. I've accompanied this with a typical local rice pilaf flavoured with leeks, broad beans and dill, and a yogurt and cucumber salad called cacik. *Serves 4*

CINNAMON-GRILLED CHICKEN
WITH A BROAD BEAN, LEEK AND DILL PILAF AND CACIK
TURKEY

For the chicken

1 x 1.5-kg free-range chicken, jointed into 8 pieces

Juice 1 small lemon

2 teaspoons Aleppo pepper (see page 207)

1 teaspoon cumin seeds

10-cm piece cinnamon stick

100 g wholemilk natural yogurt

4 garlic cloves, crushed

Salt and freshly ground black pepper

For the pilaf

2 tablespoons extra virgin olive oil

1 garlic clove, crushed in a garlic press

1 medium-sized leek, trimmed, cleaned and thinly sliced

100 g fresh or frozen shelled broad beans

225 g basmati rice

400 ml *Chicken stock* (see page 211)

3 tablespoons chopped dill

For the cacik

200-g piece cucumber

250 g wholemilk natural yogurt

1 garlic clove, crushed

Take the chicken breasts off the bone and then cut each one in half. Mix the lemon juice, Aleppo pepper and 1 teaspoon salt together in a shallow dish. Add the chicken pieces, turn them over well in the mixture and leave to marinate for 20 minutes.

Meanwhile, grind the cumin seeds and cinnamon stick together in a spice grinder to a fine powder. Mix into the yogurt with the garlic. Add the yogurt marinade to the chicken and mix together well so that all the pieces of chicken get well coated. Set aside for another 20 minutes or so.

Prepare and light your charcoal brazier or barbecue and leave it to get hot. For the pilaf, heat the olive oil in a medium-sized pan, add the garlic, leek and broad beans and fry gently for 4 minutes. Add the rice and fry for another 2 minutes or until the rice starts to crackle. Add the stock and ½ teaspoon salt, bring to the boil, cover, reduce the heat to low and leave to cook for 10 minutes. Turn off the heat and leave the rice undisturbed for a further 5 minutes.

While the pilaf is cooking, thread 4 pieces of the chicken onto a pair of parallel long metal skewers – this will stop them from spinning round when you come to turn them. Do the same with the remaining 4 pieces of chicken. When the charcoal is glowing red and covered in a thick layer of white ash, suspend the skewers about 15–18 cm from the coals and cook for 10–12 minutes, turning every now and then, until the chicken is cooked through but not excessively browned.

Meanwhile, for the cacik, peel the cucumber, cut it in half lengthways and scoop out and discard the seeds. Cut the flesh into small dice. Stir into the yogurt with the garlic and some salt to taste.

Uncover the pilaf and fork through the dill and a little more seasoning to taste if necessary. Serve the chicken with the pilaf and cacik.

LAMB VEAL BEEF
THE WHOLE PIG

THE SCENT OF GRILLING MEAT OVER CHARCOAL,
THE COMFORT OF LONG-COOKED STEWS AND THE
PUNCHY FLAVOURS OF SAUSAGES AND OFFAL

Cap de Formentor, Mallorca

CAN THERE BE ANYTHING more exquisite than skewered cubes of lamb marinated with olive oil, lemon juice and Greek oregano and cooked over charcoal? I know people are a bit dismissive of Greek food, but when it's done right, nothing is better. I love opening out a freshly baked warm flatbread, using it as a glove to hold the chargrilled lamb while I pull the skewer out, and then making a sandwich with the tzatziki, tomatoes and pickles. A souvlaki is not dissimilar to a Turkish shish kebab. *Serves 8*

SOUVLAKI:
LAMB SOUVLAKI WITH FLATBREADS, TZATZIKI, TOMATOES AND PICKLES
CORFU

2 kg boned shoulder of lamb

2 tablespoons chopped fresh oregano or 1 tablespoon dried, **Greek if possible**

Juice 1 large lemon

150 ml extra virgin olive oil

Salt and freshly ground black pepper

For the flatbreads

350 g plain flour

1 teaspoon salt

2 teaspoons easy-blend yeast

2 tablespoons extra virgin olive oil

To serve

1 quantity *Tzatziki* (see page 23)

250 g ripe tomatoes, sliced

2 pickled cucumbers or large gherkins, thinly sliced lengthways

Mild green pickled chillies, sliced (optional)

A little paprika for sprinkling

Cut the lamb into strips and cubes, trimming away any excess fat. Put the meat into a bowl with the oregano, lemon juice, olive oil, 2 teaspoons salt and some black pepper and leave to marinate at room temperature for 1 hour.

For the flatbreads, sift the flour, salt and yeast into a bowl and make a well in the centre. Add 250 ml warm water and olive oil and mix together to make a soft dough. Transfer to a lightly floured surface and knead for 5 minutes. Put back into the bowl, cover and leave somewhere warm for about 1 hour until doubled in size.

Punch back the dough, turn it out onto a lightly floured surface and knead once more until smooth. Divide into 8 pieces and roll each one into a ball. Cover and leave to rise for 10 minutes. Meanwhile, preheat the oven to 240°C/Gas Mark 9. Working with one ball of dough at a time, roll it out flat until it is about 22 cm across. Place it on a greased baking sheet, spray lightly with a little water and bake for 2–3 minutes. Keep warm in a tea towel. Repeat for the rest of the breads.

Light your barbecue. Thread about 5 pieces of meat, folding the thinner strips in half, on to sixteen 25-cm-long metal skewers and cook, in batches if necessary, for 6 minutes, turning them 2–3 times during cooking, until they are nicely browned on the outside and cooked through but still moist and juicy in the centre. Transfer to a serving platter and keep warm while you cook the remainder.

THIS RECIPE IS BASED on one from Andy Harris's book, *Modern Greek*. Andy is a chum of mine who runs the Australian *Gourmet Traveller* magazine, and whose deep knowledge of Greece and Greek cooking has been invaluable to me. He lived in Greece for eleven years before moving to Australia. One of the truths I repeatedly learnt during the time we were filming in Corfu was that Greek food, though very simple, can be completely lovely if cooked properly. It's a shame that the average tourist doesn't get to see it. The Greeks have a robust excess with seasoning, and the use of herbs and spices in a dish such as this, long, slow-cooked lamb with plenty of lemon juice, salt, oregano and garlic, is spot-on. Serve with a green salad and plenty of fresh crusty bread. *Serves 6–8*

KLEFTIKO:

SLOW-COOKED LAMB WITH GARLIC, OREGANO, LEMON AND POTATOES

CORFU

2 x 1-kg shoulders of lamb, each one cut into 3 large
  chunks through the bone (get your butcher to do this)
2 kg waxy maincrop potatoes, such as Desiree, peeled and
  cut into 5–6-cm chunks
1 head of garlic, outside papery skins removed, cut in
  half through the middle
1 tablespoon dried oregano, Greek if possible
3–6 fresh bay leaves
2 tablespoons fresh oregano or marjoram leaves
3 tablespoons extra virgin olive oil, plus extra for drizzling
Juice 2 large lemons
Salt and freshly ground black pepper

Preheat the oven to 190°C/Gas Mark 5. Combine the meat, potatoes and garlic in a large ovenproof casserole dish. Sprinkle with the dried and fresh herbs, olive oil, lemon juice, 100 ml water, 2 teaspoons of salt and plenty of black pepper and mix together well, then nestle the pieces of meat down in among the potatoes. Drizzle with a little more oil.

Cover the casserole tightly with foil and a well-fitting lid and bake for 3 hours until the meat is falling off the bone. However, check after a couple of hours to make sure it doesn't need a little more water.

THIS IS ANOTHER of the famous celebratory dishes of Morocco, a speciality of the Berbers, the nomadic tribes of North Africa. There, a whole lamb is slowly spit-roasted over the embers of an open fire, basted continuously with butter flavoured with cumin, paprika and garlic until it is falling off the bone, and then served sprinkled with cumin-flavoured sea salt. I had this in Marrakech earlier this year. I'd been invited, with my partner Sarah, to celebrate Antonio Carluccio's seventieth birthday and my friend Andy Harris's fiftieth birthday (Andy's recipe for kleftiko appears on page 131). The mechoui was the star of that evening, and I had b'stilla (see page 155) too. The evening included belly-dancers and an ensemble of acrobats and jugglers, all set in the most delightful riad and giving a real sense of the secret life of Morocco. The next evening we went to the central square of Jemaa el Fna, famous for its street food, snake-charmers and story-tellers, where I ate tiny snails in a cumin-and-chilli-scented broth, kebabs and merguez sausages cooked over charcoal. Unbelievably, a couple of the waiters recognized me. They appeared to have learnt every TV cook's catchphrase and mannerisms off pat: Jamie Oliver, Ainsley, Antony Worrall Thompson, James Martin, Nigella, Brian Turner and me, like they'd been watching us on telly for ever. They would have picked this up from British tourists as a way of persuading others to come and eat at their food stall. Testimony to the business acumen of the average Moroccan street-trader. I promised to send them one of my books, and I did. *Serves 6*

MECHOUI: SLOW-ROASTED GARLIC AND CUMIN-SPICED LAMB
MOROCCO

1 whole shoulder of lamb on the bone, weighing about 2.75 kg
2 fat garlic cloves, crushed
1 tablespoon cumin seeds, freshly ground
1½ teaspoons sweet paprika
50 g butter, softened

Sea salt and freshly ground black pepper

For the cumin and sea salt seasoning
1 tablespoon cumin seeds
1 tablespoon sea salt
¼ teaspoon freshly ground black pepper

Preheat the oven to 160°C/Gas Mark 3. Cut away any excess fat from the underside of the lamb, then make deep incisions all over the meat on both sides.

Mix the garlic, cumin, paprika and butter together with 1 teaspoon salt and spread this all over the meat, working it down well into all the little slits.

Place the lamb, skinned-side up, on a shallow trivet in the base of large roasting tin, and roast for 4 hours, basting it every 30 minutes with the buttery juices from the tin, until it is well coloured on the outside but still juicy on the inside. This will give you meltingly tender lamb. If you would like it to be falling off the bone, cover the top of the lamb loosely with a sheet of foil and cook it for a further hour.

Meanwhile, for the cumin and sea salt seasoning, heat a small, dry frying pan over a high heat and as soon as it is hot, add the cumin seeds and shake them around for a few seconds until they darken slightly and start to smell aromatic. Tip them into a mortar and grind them slightly with the pestle, but don't render them to a fine powder. Stir in the sea salt and pepper and tip the mixture into a small shallow bowl.

Remove the meat from the bone and break it into small chunks. Arrange the lamb on a warmed serving platter and serve at once with the cumin and sea salt seasoning for sprinkling.

THIS RECIPE WAS GIVEN to me by Lahcen Bequi, who runs a cookery school in Fes. He started cooking when he was just ten, when his parents sent him away to school in a town a fair distance away from the Berber village in the High Atlas mountains in which he grew up. It was amazing for me to talk to this intelligent and gifted cook, knowing that he'd spent his childhood out in the high pastures shepherding sheep and goats. A tagine is historically a Berber dish and it seemed to me, tasting this one with lamb and prunes, that I was eating the real thing. The meat was meltingly soft, and this, above all dishes, convinced me of the sophistication of the Moroccan use of fruit and nuts with meat. It had a beguiling smokiness about it. He took an immense time to cook it, and explained in detail that the importance of the shape of the tagine is that the steam inside rises to the top of the still cold conical lid, where it condenses and drips back down, bathing the meat in fragrant juices. Serve with steamed couscous, or bread. *Serves 6*

LAMB TAGINE
WITH PRUNES AND ALMONDS
MOROCCO

2 tablespoons olive oil

1 x 2-kg shoulder of lamb on the bone, cut into 6 pieces

50 g butter

1 large onion, halved and thinly sliced

1 beef tomato, sliced

1 teaspoon ground ginger

1 teaspoon ras el hanout (see page 208)

½ teaspoon saffron strands

½ teaspoon turmeric

1 small bunch coriander

1 small bunch flat-leaf parsley

1 large cinnamon stick, halved

250g prunes (not need-to-soak)

40g blanched almonds, toasted

2 tablespoons lightly toasted sesame seeds

Salt and freshly ground black pepper

Trim the excess fat from the pieces of lamb and season them well. Heat the oil in a large tagine or flameproof casserole, add the lamb pieces and brown lightly all over. Lift the meat out onto a plate, add the butter and the onions and cook, stirring, until they are soft and lightly browned.

Overlap the slices of tomato on top of the onions, followed by the pieces of lamb. Mix the ginger, ras el hanout, saffron and turmeric with 100 ml water and drizzle the mixture all over the lamb. Push the bunches of coriander and parsley and the cinnamon stick into the centre of the meat, season once more lightly with salt and pepper, and pour over enough water to almost cover the meat – about another 500 ml. Cover and leave to cook over a gentle heat for 1½ hours until

the lamb is tender. Remove the herbs.

Meanwhile, remove the stones from the prunes and replace them with some of the toasted blanched almonds. After the lamb has been cooking for 1½ hours, uncover, and skim away the excess fat from the surface of the sauce. Put the prunes in among the pieces of meat and leave to simmer a little more vigorously, uncovered, for a further 15 minutes or so until the meat is almost falling off the bone, the prunes are tender and the sauce is reduced and concentrated in flavour.

Taste the sauce and adjust the seasoning if necessary. Scatter the tagine with the remaining toasted almonds and the sesame seeds and serve immediately.

THERE IS A VERY pleasant restaurant in Maritimo de Diso, near Otranto in Puglia, called Aria Corte. Maritimo is where Lord McAlpine, one-time treasurer of the Conservative Party and good friend of Margaret Thatcher, has an extraordinary converted convent with nine wonderfully idiosyncratic rooms. He sent me down to this restaurant and asked them to give us all the local specialities. I speedily found I was in another world of Italian food, with a whole table full of vegetarian antipasti like the broad bean purée with wild chicory on page 47, and plates of courgette fritters, aubergine parmigiana and braised fennel. But the best dish that day was not vegetarian but these little fennel sausages, called luganega, stewed with waxy potatoes and lemon zest. The perfect sausages for this dish in my view are those from Fratelli Camisa (see page 212), which come in one long length, not linked like sausages from the UK. If you are using ordinary sausages, add a teaspoon of fennel seeds to the onions when frying. *Serves 4*

FENNEL SAUSAGES
BRAISED WITH LEMONY POTATOES AND BAY LEAVES
PUGLIA

450 g luganega sausages or other
   nice meaty pork chipolatas
4 tablespoons extra virgin olive oil
1 small onion, halved and thinly
   sliced
2 garlic cloves, thinly sliced
750 g small waxy potatoes, peeled
   and each cut into quarters
Pared zest and juice ½ lemon
4 fresh bay leaves
2 tablespoons chopped parsley
Salt and freshly ground black
   pepper

Preheat the oven to 180°C/Gas Mark 4. Twist the sausages into 7.5-cm lengths and then separate into individual sausages. Heat 1 tablespoon of the oil in a 26-cm shallow flameproof casserole dish. Add the sausages and fry until nicely browned all over. Lift onto a plate and set aside.

Add the onion, garlic and another tablespoon of oil to the casserole and fry until soft and lightly golden. Stir in the potatoes, sausages, lemon zest and juice, bay leaves, half the chopped parsley, ½ teaspoon salt and 10 turns of the black pepper mill. Pour over the rest of the oil along with 120 ml water, cover tightly with the lid and bake for 30–40 minutes until the potatoes are tender. Remove the lemon zest and sprinkle with the rest of the parsley before serving.

THIS IS ANOTHER RECIPE inspired by a visit to Rouvas restaurant in Corfu Town. I have a great affection for these Mediterranean baked dishes of meat, pasta, tomato and cheese, and in Corfu they give their version a unique quality with kefalotiri cheese and cinnamon. Kefalotiri is a dry, firm, ewe's milk cheese, full of irregular holes, which ranges in colour from white through to pale yellow, depending on the grazing of the sheep. It is fresh and slightly sharp-tasting, with a distinct flavour of ewe's milk. Just suppose you belong to a book club, and you need an all-in-one simple dish to feed everyone, because you know that with book clubs, you shouldn't try too hard with the food. This is perfection: pastitsio, green salad, crusty bread and gutsy red wine. You will all then have the strength to discuss the latest Ian McEwan. *Serves 8–10*

PASTITSIO:
BEEF AND MACARONI PIE WITH CINNAMON, RED WINE AND KEFALOTIRI CHEESE
CORFU

500 g tubular pasta, such as rigatoni, tubetti or tortiglioni

2 eggs, lightly beaten

50 g finely grated Greek kefalotiri cheese or parmesan cheese

2 tablespoons melted butter

10 g fresh white breadcrumbs

For the white sauce

115 g butter

115 g plain flour

1.2 litres full-cream milk, plus a little extra

½ teaspoon freshly grated nutmeg

For the meat sauce

4 tablespoons olive oil

1 medium onion, finely chopped

4 garlic cloves, finely chopped

2 celery sticks, finely chopped

1 kg lean minced beef

200 ml red wine

400-g can chopped tomatoes

2 tablespoons tomato purée

10-cm piece cinnamon stick

¼ teaspoon ground cloves

1 tablespoon dried oregano, Greek if possible

2 tablespoons fresh chopped oregano

3 fresh bay leaves

Salt and freshly ground black pepper

For the meat sauce, heat the olive oil in a medium-sized pan, add the onion, garlic and celery and fry until just beginning to brown. Add the minced beef and fry over a high heat for 3–4 minutes, breaking up any lumps with the wooden spoon as it browns. Add the red wine, tomatoes, tomato purée, cinnamon stick, ground cloves, dried and fresh oregano, bay leaves, 100 ml water, 1½ teaspoons salt and some black pepper, and simmer for 30–40 minutes, stirring now and then, until the sauce has thickened but is still nicely moist. Remove and discard the cinnamon stick and bay leaves.

Bring 4.5 litres water to the boil in a large saucepan with 8 teaspoons salt. Add the pasta and cook until *al dente* – about 13 minutes, but take care not to overcook as it will cook a little further in the oven. Drain well, transfer to a large bowl and leave to cool slightly.

For the white sauce, melt the butter in a medium-sized non-stick saucepan, add the flour and cook, stirring, over a medium heat, for 1 minute. Gradually beat in the milk, then bring to the boil, stirring, lower the heat and leave to simmer for 5–7 minutes, stirring occasionally.

Season with the nutmeg and some salt and pepper to taste.

Preheat the oven to 180°C/Gas Mark 4. Stir 250 ml (about one-fifth) of the white sauce into the warm pasta with the beaten eggs and half the grated cheese. Keep the remaining sauce warm over a low heat, stirring now and then and adding more milk if it begins to get a little thick.

Use the melted butter to grease a large, shallow ovenproof dish that measures about 23 x 33 cm across and 7 cm deep. Spread one-third of the pasta over the base of the dish and cover with half the meat sauce. Add another third of the pasta and then the rest of the meat sauce, then cover with a final layer of pasta. Spoon over the remaining white sauce. Mix the remaining grated cheese with the breadcrumbs and sprinkle them over the top. Bake for 40 minutes until bubbling hot and golden brown.

FAR FROM BEING a pale copy of Italian canelloni, Barcelona canalons – which use no tomato sauce, just plenty of unctuous béchamel – are justifiably the most popular dish in Barcelona. *Serves 6*

CANALONS A LA BARCELONESA:
BARCELONA CANALONS STUFFED WITH CHICKEN LIVERS, MINCED VEAL AND SERRANO HAM
CATALONIA

4 tablespoons extra virgin olive oil

1 medium onion, chopped

1 garlic clove, crushed

175 g minced pork

175 g minced veal

150 g fresh free-range chicken livers, finely chopped

75 g thickly sliced serrano ham, finely chopped

20 g fresh white breadcrumbs

1 medium egg, lightly beaten

2 tablespoons finely grated

mature manchego or parmesan cheese

2 tablespoons chopped flat-leaf parsley

½ teaspoon freshly grated nutmeg

12 sheets fresh egg lasagne

Butter, for greasing

Salt and freshly ground black pepper

For the béchamel sauce

1 small onion, peeled and halved

6 cloves

900 ml full-cream milk

4 bay leaves

1 teaspoon black peppercorns

60 g butter

60 g plain flour

4 tablespoons double cream

Freshly grated nutmeg

Freshly ground white pepper

3 tablespoons finely grated mature manchego or parmesan cheese

For the béchamel sauce, stud the onion with the cloves and put into a pan with the milk, bay leaves and peppercorns. Bring the milk to the boil and set it aside for 20 minutes to infuse.

For the filling, heat the oil in a large frying pan, add the onion and cook over a medium heat, stirring frequently, for 6–7 minutes until the onions are very soft and a golden brown. Add the garlic and cook for a further 2 minutes. Add the pork, veal and chicken livers and cook for 4–5 minutes, breaking up the minced pork and veal with a wooden spoon as they brown. Add the ham and cook for a further 2 minutes until softened. Leave to simmer, uncovered, for 3–4 minutes, then remove from the heat and cool slightly. Stir the breadcrumbs into the meat mixture with the egg, cheese, parsley, nutmeg and some salt and pepper to taste.

Bring 4.5 litres water to the boil in a large saucepan with 8 teaspoons salt. Drop in the sheets of lasagne pasta, one at a time, take the pan off the heat and leave them to soak for 5 minutes. Drain well, leave to cool slightly and then separate the sheets.

Spoon some of the meat filling along one short edge of each lasagne sheet and roll up. Lay side by side, seam-side down, in a well-buttered 25 x 30 cm shallow ovenproof dish.

Preheat the oven to 200°C/Gas Mark 6. To make the béchamel sauce, bring the milk back to the boil, then strain into a jug. Melt the butter in a non-stick pan, add the flour and cook over a medium heat for 1 minute. Gradually beat in the milk, bring to the boil, stirring, and leave to simmer gently over a low heat for 5 minutes. Remove from the heat and stir in the cream, nutmeg and some salt and white pepper to taste. Pour the sauce evenly over the canalons and sprinkle with the cheese. Bake for 25–30 minutes until golden and bubbling.

INTERESTINGLY, a number of my friends who are not fond of offal found this dish extremely tasty, which seems to me to prove a point. It is the idea of offal and not the taste that people object to. The result here is not particularly intense but rather a lovely vegetable dish with a savoury background. *Serves 6*

Sa Pobla, Mallorca

FRITTO MALLORQUINA:
SAUTÉED POTATOES, PEPPERS AND PEAS WITH LAMB'S LIVER, KIDNEYS AND SPRING ONIONS

MALLORCA

750 g lamb's offal (an equal mixture of hearts, kidneys and liver)
200 ml olive oil
6 garlic cloves, chopped
500 g waxy potatoes, such as Charlotte, peeled and cut into 1-cm pieces

1 small cauliflower, about 450 g, cut into tiny florets
3 artichoke hearts, cut into 1-cm pieces, or 4 baby artichokes cut into quarters
1 large red pepper, seeded and cut into 1-cm dice
½ teaspoon peperoncino or

crushed dried chillies
1 bunch fat spring onions, trimmed and sliced
100 g shelled or frozen peas
A good handful of fennel herb, roughly chopped
Salt and freshly ground black pepper

Halve the kidneys and snip out the cores with scissors. Cut the kidneys, hearts and liver into 1-cm pieces.

Heat 3 tablespoons of the oil in a large frying pan. Add the garlic and potatoes and fry over a medium heat for 10 minutes until they are soft and golden. Season with a little salt and pepper, spoon onto a plate and keep warm. Add another 2 tablespoons oil to the pan, add the cauliflower and artichokes and season with a little salt and pepper. Cover and cook for 15 minutes or until the cauliflower is tender. Set aside with the potatoes. Add another tablespoon oil to the pan with the red pepper and fry for 5–6 minutes until tender.

Meanwhile, heat 4 tablespoons oil in a large, 40-cm frying pan, add the peperoncino and the prepared offal and cook for 5 minutes, until lightly browned and the excess juices have evaporated. Season with salt and pepper.

Tip the fried garlic and potatoes, cauliflower and artichokes, and red pepper into the pan with the offal and mix together well. Place over a low heat and reheat gently.

Add the rest of the oil to a smaller frying pan with the spring onions and peas and cook for 1–2 minutes until tender. Tip into the larger pan, add the fennel herb and toss everything together. Serve straight away.

THE IDEA FOR THIS RECIPE came from a very enjoyable lunch we had at a farm on the outskirts of Oliena in the centre of Sardinia. Costantino Puggioni was an expert in slow-cooking suckling pig over a mountain-herb-strewn wood fire. It's a long process, involving basting the beast with flaming bacon fat to make the skin crisper. Much as I would like to recommend your purchasing a whole suckling pig, sadly, this is not going to happen for the average reader, so I've written a version incorporating some of the flavours of Sardinia with slow-roasted belly pork instead. The secret to getting crisp and yet still delicate crackling is to buy belly pork that has a lot of fat under the skin, which you'll get from a good butcher. In case this is hard to get hold of, I've added a method of carefully grilling the pork skin-side up at the end of roasting to crisp it if it needs it. I suggest mashed potatoes and some cabbage as accompaniments. *Serves 6*

BELLY OF PORK, SLOW ROASTED
WITH FENNEL SEEDS, GARLIC AND ROSEMARY
SARDINIA

2-kg piece thick unskinned belly pork, from a
　nice fatty pig, bones removed

2 teaspoons fennel seeds

1 tablespoon black peppercorns

A large pinch of crushed dried chillies

1 tablespoon sea salt flakes or 2 teaspoons
　coarse sea salt

3 large garlic cloves, crushed

Leaves from 18-cm rosemary sprig

2 tablespoons extra virgin olive oil

2 large onions, halved and thinly sliced

Salt and freshly ground black pepper

For the gravy

3 tablespoons Cabernet Sauvignon or other red
　wine vinegar

1 teaspoon plain flour

For the carrots

750 g large carrots, peeled, or 750 g baby new
　carrots, topped and tailed and scraped clean

600 ml apple juice

2 teaspoons caster sugar

30 g butter

2 teaspoons cider vinegar

A large handful of flat-leaf parsley leaves, chopped

Put the fennel seeds, peppercorns and crushed chillies into a mortar and coarsely grind with the pestle. Then add the salt, garlic and rosemary leaves and grind everything together into a coarse paste. Mix in the oil. Place the belly pork skin-side down on a board and make a series of shallow cuts into the flesh. Spread the paste over the meat and push it down well into the cuts. Leave it somewhere cool for at least 1 hour, or overnight in the fridge.

　Preheat the oven to 160°C/Gas Mark 3. Spread the onions over the base of a large roasting tin. Turn the pork skin-side up, place it on a rack and rest it over the top of the onions. Rub the skin well with oil and then sprinkle with salt. Pour 600 ml water into the tin and roast the pork for 2¼ –2½ hours until very tender.

　While the pork is roasting, if using large carrots cut them into slices approximately 10 mm thick and then cut each slice across into 3–4 chunky matchsticks. Use baby carrots whole. Put the whole or chopped carrots into a wide, shallow pan and cover with the apple juice. Add ½ teaspoon salt, the sugar, butter and vinegar. Bring to the boil and leave to simmer vigorously

for about 30 minutes until the carrots are just tender. There will still be some liquid left at this stage. Remove from the heat and set aside. Keep warm.

Remove the pork from the oven and increase the oven temperature to 230°C/Gas Mark 8. Return the pork on its rack to the top shelf of the oven but keep the roasting tin of onions out to make the gravy. Roast the pork for a further 15 to 20 minutes until the skin is crisp.

For the gravy, you need the onions in the roasting tin to be nicely coloured. If they are not quite brown enough, place the roasting tin directly over a medium heat and cook them for a few minutes longer until they have caramelized. Then pour the excess fat away from the tin, place it back over a medium heat and add the vinegar and about 50 ml water. Rub the base of the tin with a wooden spoon to release all the caramelized cooking juices, then stir in the flour, followed by another 250 ml water and bring to the boil. Pass through a sieve into a small, clean pan and leave to simmer until reduced to a well-flavoured gravy. Season to taste with salt and keep hot.

When the pork has finished roasting, remove it from the oven. If the skin is only crisp in patches, turn on your grill to high. Slide the pork under the grill so that it is about 15 cm away from the heat and carefully grill the skin side, turning it round as necessary as each area starts to puff up, for 2–3 minutes. The object is to crisp the skin but not burn it or bubble it up excessively.

Return the carrots to the heat and cook rapidly over a high heat until the remaining liquid has reduced and they are covered in a sweet, buttery glaze. Stir in the parsley and adjust the seasoning if necessary.

Because the pork will be well cooked and very tender, turn the piece over onto the skin side and cut through the flesh first and then the skin, to make the carving easier. Aim to give each person 2 thick slices. Serve with the gravy poured over and a generous spoonful of carrots, and of course mashed potato and some cabbage if you wish.

I REALLY ENJOYED my day at Vincent Tabarani's cookery school just outside Bastia. He's one of the most distinguished chefs on the island but refreshingly lacking in arrogance, and the school was well equipped with good quality stoves, chopping boards, knives and rugged casseroles for hearty Corsican cooking. And the students, all a little older than me, were good fun and really enjoying themselves. He cooked two dishes: roast kid with cocos roses (the French name for borlotti beans), and roasted milk-fed lamb with roasted figs and tomatoes. He gave us this recipe, in which he used a gigot of kid goat, but I've adapted it to lamb instead and I've taken the tomatoes from the other dish he made and served them with this one. *Serves 6*

VINCENT TABARANI'S
ROAST KNUCKLE OF LAMB WITH ROSEMARY AND BORLOTTI BEANS
CORSICA

1.5 kg half leg of lamb, knuckle end

50 ml olive oil

3 garlic cloves, crushed

1 small onion, thinly sliced

1 medium carrot, thinly sliced

100 ml dry white wine

200 ml water or stock

1 teaspoon chopped parsley

Salt and freshly ground black pepper

For the beans

400 g dried borlotti beans, soaked overnight

1 bouquet garni of bay leaves, thyme, parsley and celery

1 rosemary sprig

1 small onion, peeled and left whole

3 garlic cloves, peeled and left whole

For the roasted tomatoes

6 ripe tomatoes, halved

1 teaspoon thyme leaves

Leaves from 1 small rosemary sprig, finely chopped

1 large garlic clove, crushed in a press

Extra virgin olive oil, for drizzling

Nonza, Corsica

Bone out the half leg of lamb (or get your butcher to do it for you) and then roll up the meat into a tidy cylindrical joint, securing it where necessary with a small fine skewer, and tie in place along its length with string. Weigh the joint and calculate the cooking time, allowing 18 minutes per 500 g. Reserve the bones and any trimmings for cooking the meat. Rub the meat with a little olive oil and season well all over.

Drain the soaked beans and put them into a saucepan with the bouquet garni, rosemary sprig, onion and garlic. Cover with 1.5 litres cold water, bring to the boil, skimming off any scum as it rises to the surface, and leave to simmer over a low heat until the beans are tender – about 1 hour. Add 1 teaspoon salt 10 minutes before the end of cooking time.

Meanwhile, preheat the oven to 200°C/Gas Mark 6. Cover the bottom of a small roasting tin with the reserved bones and trimmings, garlic, onion and carrot. Put the prepared lamb on top and roast for 55 minutes.

Put the tomatoes cut-side up into a lightly oiled, shallow baking dish and sprinkle with the thyme leaves, rosemary, garlic and some salt and pepper, then drizzle with olive oil. Bake along-side the lamb for 25–30 minutes or until tender.

Remove the lamb from the oven and switch it off. Lift the meat onto a plate, cover tightly with foil and return to the oven to keep warm, along with the tomatoes.

Put the roasting tin over a high heat, add the bouquet garni from the beans and press out all the flavour. Then add the white wine and rub the base of the tin with a wooden spoon to release all the caramelized juices. Add the water or stock and leave to simmer until reduced by half. Pass the juices through a fine sieve into a medium-sized pan, adjust the seasoning and return to a low heat.

Drain the beans, discard the aromatic flavourings and add the beans to the pan of roasting juices. Heat them through over a low heat.

Carve the lamb across into slices. Stir the carving juices into the beans and then spoon them onto a warmed serving platter. Sprinkle the beans with the chopped parsley, lay the meat on top and serve straight away with the roasted tomatoes.

DAVID PRITCHARD, the director, and I are both occasionally so overwhelmed by the energy, vitality and sense of theatre of a food event that we think it should be the setting for an opera. The restaurant of Imam Cagdas in Gaziantep was one such place. It was a large and enormously busy restaurant turning out an array of tender, aromatic, charcoal-imbued kebabs, and these lahmacun. This was food more influenced by the lifestyle of central Asia than the Mediterranean: dishes that could be cooked by nomadic tribes on the move. As soon as you arrive, you are served with warm, fresh lavash, the thin, crisp, local flatbread; a bowl of ayran, a drink made of water, natural yogurt and a pinch of salt; salad dressed with pomegranate molasses, and these lahmacun, which you fill with a fistful of fresh parsley, sprinkle with lemon juice and roll up to eat. In the space of 45 minutes, 20 or 30 chefs and waiters must have served about 300 people. This is fast food at its best. Just make sure to roll the dough thinly, spread the lamb topping right out to the edges and cook it quickly in a very hot oven. *Makes 12*

LAHMACUN:
SPICY MINCED LAMB FLATBREADS
TURKEY

1 quantity *Flatbread dough* (see page 210)

For the topping

600 g lean minced lamb

1 medium onion

200 g (about ½ each) red and green pepper, stalks and seeds removed

1 garlic clove, crushed

15 g flat-leaf parsley leaves, chopped

1½ teaspoons Aleppo pepper (see page 207)

Salt

Flat-leaf parsley sprigs and lemon wedges, to serve

Make the dough according the instructions on page 210. Meanwhile, for the topping, bring the minced lamb back to room temperature if necessary. Roughly chop the onion, red pepper and green pepper, put them into a food processor and process, using the pulse button, until finely chopped but not a pulp. Tip into a sieve set over a bowl and press out the excess liquid. Add to the minced lamb with the crushed garlic, chopped parsley, Aleppo pepper and 2 teaspoons salt. Mix together into a soft paste using your hands. Divide the mixture into 12.

Preheat the oven to 240°C/Gas Mark 9. Punch back the dough, turn it out onto a lightly floured surface and knead once more until smooth. Divide the dough into 12 evenly sized pieces. Working with 4 pieces at a time, roll each one out very thinly on a lightly floured surface into ovals of 14 x 24 cm. Place side by side on 2 lightly floured baking sheets.

Using your fingertips, spread one portion of the lamb mixture evenly over each base, taking it right up to the edges because the mixture shrinks as it cooks. Bake for 8 minutes until the dough is lightly browned. Serve straight away. The traditional way to do this is to pile a few parsley sprigs towards one end of the flatbread, squeeze over a little lemon juice and roll it up, much like you would a taco. While your guests start to eat, repeat with the remaining dough and lamb topping. This is one of those dishes where the cook always eats last.

RABBIT
PARTRIDGE
QUAIL
WILD BOAR

Meat from the small dry islands
has tended to be scarce, hence the
popularity of furred and feathered
game from the hills

Bonifacio, Corsica

THIS IS ANOTHER DISH to cook in the *mangal*: see the Cinnamon-grilled chicken on page 124. It also uses a similar double-marinating technique: first in lemon juice, then in yogurt. Aleppo pepper (see page 207) is not very hot, so if you are using any other type of hot red pepper instead, such as hot paprika, pimentón picante, crushed chilli flakes or cayenne pepper, add it gradually, and to taste. If you are able to get all this right, the smell and taste of these marinated quail will be something special. To make your own flatbreads to serve alongside, see page 210. *Serves 4*

GRILLED QUAIL
WITH A YOGURT, GARLIC, CHILLI PEPPER AND ZAHTAR MARINADE
TURKEY

8 prepared large quail

Juice ½ lemon

2 teaspoons Aleppo pepper, plus extra for sprinkling

100 g wholemilk natural yogurt

3 garlic cloves, crushed

3 tablespoons olive oil

1 teaspoon tomato purée

2 teaspoons zahtar (see page 208), plus extra for serving

Sea salt flakes, salt and freshly ground black pepper

For the spicy onion and tomato salad (ezme)

½ green pepper, stalk and seeds removed

100 g piece of cucumber, peeled, halved lengthways and seeds removed

1 small onion, halved

2 large, ripe juicy tomatoes, skinned, or 225 g canned plum tomatoes

1 garlic clove, crushed

2 tablespoons extra virgin olive oil

1½ teaspoons red wine vinegar

½ teaspoon Aleppo pepper

1 small bunch flat-leaf parsley, chopped

Leaves from 2 mint sprigs, finely chopped

Fresh flatbread, to serve

To spatchcock the quail, turn them breast-side down, then cut along both sides of the backbone with kitchen scissors and remove it. Open the bird out, turn it over and press down firmly on the breastbone until it lies flat. Then make a small slash in the breast of each one to allow the marinade to penetrate. Place the quail in a large shallow dish.

Pour the lemon juice over the quail, turn over once so they are well coated, then sprinkle 1 teaspoon of the Aleppo pepper and ½ teaspoon salt all over the birds. Set aside for 15–20 minutes.

Meanwhile, mix the yogurt with the garlic, olive oil, tomato purée, the zahtar, the rest of the Aleppo pepper, another ½ teaspoon salt and some freshly ground black pepper. Drain away the excess lemon juice from the quail, add the yogurt mixture and rub it well into both sides of each bird. Cover and leave to marinate for 30 minutes to 1 hour, but don't be tempted to leave it any longer or the acids in the yogurt will make the flesh go too soft.

For the spicy onion and tomato salad (ezme), finely chop the green pepper, cucumber, onion and tomatoes by hand. Mix them together in a bowl with the crushed garlic, tip the mixture into a large sieve and leave until most of the excess liquid has drained away. When it has reached a firm

consistency, transfer to a bowl and stir in the oil, vinegar, Aleppo pepper, parsley, mint, ½ teaspoon salt and some freshly ground black pepper. Set aside for the flavour to intensify.

Preheat a charcoal barbecue over which to cook the quail (see page 124) and leave until any flames have died down and the glowing coals are covered in a thick layer of white ash – this will take anything up to 30 minutes. The important thing is not to have it too searingly hot or the quail will burn and you will lose the flavour of the marinade. They are better to be cooked gently.

Lift the quail out of the marinade and thread them through the side onto 2 parallel skewers. This will keep them flat and prevent them from spinning round during cooking. Suspend them, in batches if necessary, over the glowing coals, and sprinkle the skin side with a little more Aleppo pepper and a few sea salt flakes. Cook for 4–5 minutes on each side, depending on the heat of the barbecue, until just cooked through and lightly coloured here and there but not excessively browned. Slide off the skewers onto warmed plates and sprinkle lightly with a little more zahtar. Serve with a little bowl of *ezme* salad alongside, and plenty of flatbread.

DEBBIE MAJOR, who works with me on all my books, is a bit of a magpie, tucking away little snippets of recipes, so much so that she can't always remember where they came from. The idea here was to use some roasted grapes with a game bird like partridge, and serve it with a gravy made with a sweet Pugliese vin santo. It seemed to me to be a perfect way to prepare and serve southern Italian game. I bet that, like the French who have that dish of pigeon and peas and say, 'The pigeons eat the peas, and we eat the peas and the pigeons,' in Puglia they say, 'The partridges eat the grapes and we eat the partridges and the grapes.' *Serves 4*

ROASTED PARTRIDGE
WITH VIN SANTO AND ROASTED GRAPES ON LIVER CROSTINI
PUGLIA

2 tablespoons olive oil, plus ½ teaspoon

50 g diced pancetta

5 garlic cloves, unpeeled

A pinch of fennel seeds

6 fresh sage leaves

4 oven-ready partridges, each weighing about 375 g, plus the livers

100 ml vin santo, marsala or sweet sherry

200 g sweet seedless red grapes

200 ml *Chicken stock* (see page 211)

1 teaspoon *Beurre manié* (see page 211)

Salt and freshly ground black pepper

For the liver crostini

4 tablespoons olive oil

4 small slices country-style bread

15 g butter

50 g fresh free-range chicken livers, cut into pieces the same size as the partridge livers

1 small garlic clove, finely chopped

Leaves from a thyme sprig

A pinch of ground mace or freshly grated nutmeg

Preheat the oven to 220°C/Gas Mark 7. Heat 2 tablespoons of the oil in small roasting tin over a medium heat, add the pancetta, garlic, fennel seeds and sage and fry for 1½–2 minutes until they just start to colour. Add the partridges and turn them over once or twice in the mixture, then leave them to take on a little colour on either side of the breast. Turn the birds breast-side up, pour over the vin santo and season them well with salt and black pepper. Transfer them to the oven and roast for 20–25 minutes, depending on how pink you like the meat.

Meanwhile, put the grapes into a non-stick shallow roasting tin or baking tray, drizzle with ½ teaspoon of oil, mix together well with your hands to coat, then sprinkle with a little salt and pepper. After the partridges have been cooking for 5 minutes, add the grapes to the oven and roast for 15–20 minutes until lightly caramelized.

While the partridges and grapes are roasting, prepare the crostini. Heat half the olive oil in a large frying pan over a medium-high heat, add the slices of bread and fry for 1 minute on each side until golden. Leave to drain on kitchen paper and keep warm.

Remove the partridges from the oven and switch it off. Lift the partridges onto an ovenproof plate, cover with some foil and return to the oven to keep warm, alongside the grapes. Place the roasting tin over a medium-high heat, add the chicken stock and rub the base of the tin with a wooden spoon to release all the caramelized juices. Leave to simmer quite vigorously until reduced by about half and well flavoured. Strain into a small pan, bring back to a simmer and whisk in the beurre manié a little at a time until you have a sauce with a good consistency. Adjust the seasoning if necessary and keep warm.

Heat the remaining oil and butter in a small frying pan, add the partridge and chicken livers, garlic and thyme leaves and sauté briskly over a high heat for 1 minute until the livers are nicely browned on the outside but still pink and juicy in the centre. Remove the pan from the heat, season the livers with the mace or nutmeg and some salt and pepper and mash to a coarse purée with a fork. Spread the livers onto the crostini and place them into the centre of 4 warmed plates.

Place one partridge on top of each crostini and scatter around some of the roasted grapes. Pour over some of the vin santo sauce and serve.

THE INSPIRATION FOR THIS DISH was the mountain sausage common everywhere in Corsica called figatellu. It's a pig's liver sausage, lightly smoked and then air-dried, and is a remarkably distinctive flavour in much of their cooking. Unfortunately at present it is utterly impossible to buy in the UK, so I've made this with the next best thing in terms of pungency of flavour: chorizo. But the other ingredients are important too. Game, in particular wild boar, is a major part of Corsican cuisine, and the wild mushrooms and chestnuts are found everywhere in this mountainous island. Stews like this are sometimes served with chestnut pulenda, a type of porridge made from chestnut flour, but I think it is better served with some buttery polenta, cooked pasta or mashed potatoes. *Serves 6*

WILD BOAR STEW
WITH WILD MUSHROOMS, CHESTNUTS AND CHORIZO
CORSICA

1.5 kg boneless shoulder of wild boar or
   pork

For the marinade

2 bay leaves

4 large thyme sprigs

3 x 18-cm rosemary sprigs

1 fat celery stick, roughly chopped

300 ml gutsy red wine, such as a Cabernet
   Sauvignon or the local Niellucciu

8 cloves

2 medium onions, sliced

6 garlic cloves, lightly crushed

12 black peppercorns

1 tablespoon juniper berries, lightly crushed

For the stew

4 tablespoons extra virgin olive oil

200 g small chorizo sausage or figatellu,
   cut into slices 4–5 mm thick

2 teaspoons tomato purée

2 teaspoons plain flour

100 ml red vermouth, such as the local
   Cap Corse

450 ml *Beef stock* (see page 211)

50 g dried porcini mushrooms

200 g vacuum-packed cooked and peeled
   chestnuts

15 g butter

200 g mixed wild mushrooms, including
   some chanterelles, wiped clean and sliced
   if large

Salt and freshly ground black pepper

Chopped parsley, to garnish

Cut the wild boar into 5-cm chunks and put the pieces in a large bowl. Add all the ingredients for the marinade, mix together well, cover and leave to marinate in the fridge for 24 hours, giving it a stir every now and then.

The next day, tip the marinated meat into a colander set over another bowl, in which to collect the wine, and leave to drain well.

Separate the pieces of meat from the rest of the marinade ingredients. Heat half the oil in a large, flameproof casserole and fry the meat in batches until it is nicely browned all over,

seasoning as you go and adding a little more oil if needed. Return all the meat to the casserole, with a little more oil if necessary, add the chorizo or figatellu and fry for a minute or two until lightly golden. Add the remaining marinade ingredients from the colander and fry until soft and richly browned. Stir in the tomato purée and fry for another minute. Stir in the flour, followed by the red vermouth, the reserved wine from the marinade, the beef stock, the porcini mushrooms, 1 teaspoon salt and 10 turns of the black pepper mill. Bring to the boil, cover with a tight-fitting lid and leave to simmer gently for 1–1½ hours.

Add the chestnuts to the casserole, replace the cover and cook for another 20–30 minutes or until the meat is very tender.

Shortly before the stew is ready, heat the butter in a large frying pan, add the mushrooms and some seasoning and fry briskly over a high heat for 1–2 minutes. Stir them into the casserole, sprinkle with the parsley and serve.

THIS RECIPE CAME FROM one of those Sardinian towns you would probably never go to. Indeed, I would never have gone to Oliena were it not for the fact that we wanted to film a bakery where they made music paper bread (*pane carasau*). This is a unique bread, made from semolina flour and water, which is rolled out like a pizza and baked in a brick oven. When puffed up, it is removed, split in half and cooked again until the thin layers are brittle and crisp. It is traditionally served sprinkled with olive oil, rosemary, salt and pepper, but is also layered in a dish with lamb broth, tomato sauce and pecorino cheese to make *pane frattau*, a kind of lasagne. This is an interesting point, because if tourists like myself went to places like Oliena regularly, it would become increasingly hard to find the local food that pays no heed to international requirements. We had the *pane frattau*, fresh gnocchi with saffron and wild asparagus, a sublime ravioli stuffed with pecorino, and this. The chef who cooked it at CK's restaurant and bar, Tonina Biseu, was a typically passionate woman who stood for no nonsense in her kitchen. She has written a cookery book in which she says, 'You must look to the past to create the dishes of the future.' *Serves 4*

BAKED PHEASANT
AND POTATOES WITH MOUNTAIN HERBS
SARDINIA

2 oven-ready pheasants
150 ml olive oil
3–4 fresh thyme sprigs
Leaves from 2 x 18-cm rosemary sprigs
A handful of fresh mint leaves
5 sage leaves, shredded
1 tablespoon dried oregano

1 kg waxy potatoes such as Charlotte, peeled and cut lengthways into segments – quarters or halves, depending on their size
2 fat garlic cloves, chopped
500 g small onions, cut into quarters
Salt and freshly ground black pepper

Preheat the oven to 200°C/Gas Mark 6. First joint the pheasants. Pull the legs away from the body, cut through the skin attaching them to the body, then pull the leg further away until the thigh joint snaps. Turn the bird over and feel along the backbone for the soft oysters of meat. Cut under the oysters with the tip of the knife and remove them with the legs. Remove the breasts by cutting them away from the ribcage, keeping the knife as close to the bones as possible, and cutting round the wishbone when you get to it. Season all the pheasant pieces lightly on both sides with salt and pepper.

Drizzle the bottom of a large, shallow casserole dish with some of the olive oil and sprinkle it with about one third of the herbs, ½ teaspoon salt and 10 turns of the black pepper mill. Add half the potatoes, turn them over in the oil and herbs and then spread them out in an even layer. Cover the potatoes with the pieces of pheasant and scatter over the garlic and onions. Sprinkle with another ½ teaspoon salt and some pepper and another third of the herbs, then cover with the rest of the potatoes. Sprinkle with the remaining herbs, a final ½ teaspoon salt and some pepper, and then drizzle over the rest of the olive oil.

Cover with a tight-fitting lid and bake in the oven for 1 hour or until the pheasant is tender.

I HAD ALWAYS BEEN a bit puzzled by this dish. The idea of sugar with meat didn't appeal, but in Fes my opinion was changed. I met an interesting Australian author there called Sandy McCutcheon, whose cook, Sanae, made this for us. I realized that b'stilla, and dishes like it, are probably what our mincemeat was like in medieval Britain before fashions changed and we took the meat out. This is normally served as a first course, cut into thin slices or small wedges, served with a little dressed green salad. *Serves 12–16*

B'STILLA: PIGEON, EGG AND ALMOND PIE WITH CINNAMON AND SUGAR

MOROCCO

125 ml olive oil

2 large onions, thinly sliced

½ teaspoon turmeric

2 teaspoons ground ginger

1 small bunch flat-leaf parsley, tied with string

8 pigeon breasts, or 4 x 175-g oven-ready pigeons

1 dozen medium eggs

Pinch of saffron strands

6 teaspoons ground cinnamon

5 tablespoons icing sugar

About 300 g filo pastry

150 g butter, melted

300 g almonds, toasted and finely chopped

Salt and freshly ground black pepper

In a large saucepan or casserole, heat half the oil. Add the onions and cook gently until soft but not browned. Add the turmeric, ginger, 1 teaspoon each black pepper and salt and fry for 2 minutes. Add the parsley and pigeons to the onion along with the rest of the oil and 300 ml water, then cover and leave to cook gently for 30–40 minutes until just cooked through and tender. Meanwhile, hard-boil 6 of the eggs, cool, then peel and roughly chop.

Uncover the dish and lift the pigeon onto a plate. Discard the parsley bunch. Leave the meat until cool enough to handle, then remove from the bones if necessary and shred it coarsely with your fingers. Cover and set aside. Discard any bones and skin.

Return the pan of cooking juices to the heat, add the saffron, 2 teaspoons of the cinnamon and 2 tablespoons of the icing sugar, and simmer rapidly until all the excess liquid has evaporated. Beat the remaining eggs, add them to the pan and cook gently until scrambled and the mixture is thick but moist.

Preheat the oven to 200°C/Gas Mark 6. Lay 2 sheets of filo on a large buttered baking sheet, over-lapping the edges and brushing the seam with melted butter, to create a square. Repeat twice more so that the pastry is 3 layers thick. Attach one more sheet of pastry to each side of the square with more butter to make a cross. Spread half the onion and egg mixture in a 30-cm circle on top of the central square. Spread over half the pigeon meat and half the hard-boiled eggs and season lightly. Scatter over half the chopped toasted almonds and then sprinkle with 1 tablespoon sugar and 1 teaspoon ground cinnamon. Make sure the layer is level – the pie should have a flat top.

Now cover the filling with another 2 layers of buttered filo pastry and repeat the layers of filling, seasoning lightly, then cover with a single layer of buttered filo. Fold the outer sheets of filo pastry over the top of the pie, moulding them round the circle of filling and brushing with more butter, to create a flat, circular pie of about 30 cm across. Brush the top with more butter and cover with a single layer of filo, tucking the edges under for a neat finish. Brush with butter and bake for 25–30 minutes until crisp and golden brown.

Remove from the oven and leave to cool slightly. Dust the top of the pie with the remaining icing sugar and sprinkle the remaining cinnamon in thin parallel lines to create a lattice effect. Serve warm.

THIS RECIPE, or something very like it, came from a restaurant in Corfu Town called Rouvas where I got into a long conversation with the chef, Nikos. He turned out to be a New York Greek in his early twenties who had come to work in Corfu because the work was a lot easier. Noticing that he was the only chef cooking for approximately 100 covers, I was a little perplexed by this. So he pointed out that he started at 7 o'clock every morning and by 12 o'clock he had finished – because, as any Greek hand knows, once the food is cooked, it then sits in the kitchen waiting to be ordered; if you order it at 12 it's hot, and at 2.30 it's not. But it's all the sort of food that is fine either hot or at room temperature. In fact, it was lovely food, and incredibly cheap, largely I suspect thanks to the extremely sensible economy of labour. Very soon we were all squabbling over the dishes – pastitsada (a rich beef stew), pastitsio, sofrito (thin slices of veal in white wine), bianco, stifado, briam – because everything was so delicious and everyone was worried that someone else at the table was getting more than their share. We had loads of retsina, and at the end of the meal, full of bonhomie, I was moved to remark that lunches don't get much better than that. The stifado was the star of the show. Serve it with sautéed potatoes and a crisp green salad. *Serves 4*

STIFADO: A RABBIT STEW WITH CARAMELIZED ONIONS, RED WINE, CINNAMON AND CURRANTS
CORFU

1 large farmed rabbit, weighing about 1.5 kg	400-g can chopped tomatoes
6 allspice berries	5-cm piece cinnamon stick
½ teaspoon black peppercorns	6 cloves
3 tablespoons extra virgin olive oil	2 fresh bay leaves
1 tablespoon flour	50 g currants
5 garlic cloves, sliced	15 g butter
50 ml red wine vinegar	450 g small pickling onions or shallots
600 ml red wine	½ teaspoon sugar
	Salt and freshly ground black pepper

To joint the rabbit, first remove the head and discard. Cut off the back legs from either side of the tail and set aside. Cut off the tail and discard. Cut off the front legs and trim away the bony ends from each one, and set them aside with the back legs. Cut away the belly flap and ribcage from the body and discard, and cut the remaining saddle across into 4 evenly sized pieces. Season all the pieces well with salt and pepper.

Grind the allspice berries and black peppercorns together into a powder (I have an electric coffee grinder specially for doing this).

Heat the olive oil in a flameproof casserole. Dust the rabbit pieces in the flour, and knock off but reserve the excess. Add half the rabbit pieces to the casserole and fry over a medium-high heat until nicely browned on both sides. Remove to a plate and repeat with the rest of the rabbit.

Return all the rabbit to the pan with the garlic and the remaining flour and cook for

1 minute. Pour over the vinegar and leave it to bubble for a minute or two, then add the red wine, tomatoes, ground spices, cinnamon, cloves, bay leaves, currants, 1 teaspoon salt and some freshly ground black pepper. Bring to the boil, part-cover and simmer for 55 minutes or until the rabbit is very tender and the sauce has reduced.

Meanwhile, melt the butter in a medium-sized pan, add the pickling onions or shallots and the sugar and fry, shaking the pan now and then, until they are richly golden all over. Then add 2 tablespoons water, cover and cook gently for 10 minutes until tender. Uncover, raise the heat and cook more rapidly for a minute or two, shaking the pan until the onions are covered in a shiny glaze. Season with a little salt and pepper and set aside.

When the rabbit has had the required cooking time, stir in the caramelized onions and simmer for a further 5 minutes.

DRIED BEANS
GRAINS RICE
PASTA

NOWHERE ELSE IN THE WORLD
ARE BEANS AND GRAINS COOKED
IN SUCH EXCITING WAYS

Bosa, Sardinia

VITTORIO'S IS A great fish restaurant on the beach at Porto Palo near Menfi on the south coast of Sicily. Vittorio is a great friend of Giorgio Locatelli, who runs one of the best Italian restaurants in London: Locando Locatelli, in Portland Square. Vittorio's kitchen is a place where you would want to spend a lot of time because there are so many lovely things being made, happy-as-can-be gesticulating cooks and open windows overlooking the sea. I didn't have to find this dish for myself because Vittorio was so keen to tell me everything about it. That's what it's like with Italians. They want to share their boundless enthusiasm for food. The combination of the fresh porcini, tomato, chilli, white wine, parsley and some carpet-shell clams (*vongole verace*) is simply irresistible. A perfect lunch on the beach. Use chestnut mushrooms instead together with a few soaked dried porcini if you can't get hold of fresh porcini. *Serves 4*

VITTORIO'S PASTA
WITH CLAMS AND PORCINI
SICILY

5 tablespoons extra virgin olive oil

4 garlic cloves, thinly sliced

¼ teaspoon crushed dried chillies

1 mild green chilli, stalk removed and thinly sliced

225 g fresh porcini mushrooms, cleaned and thickly sliced

2 large, ripe vine tomatoes, skinned, seeded and sliced

400 g dried spaghetti

1 kg small clams, such as carpet-shell, washed

60 ml dry white wine

A large handful flat-leaf parsley, leaves finely chopped

Salt

Bring 4.5 litres water to the boil in a large saucepan with 8 teaspoons salt. Meanwhile, put the oil and garlic into a deep sauté or frying pan and place it over a medium heat. As soon as the garlic begins to sizzle round the edges, add the crushed chillies, green chilli and sliced porcini and cook briskly for 2–3 minutes. Add the tomatoes and cook for another minute or two. Set to one side and keep hot.

Add the pasta to the pan of boiling water and cook for 9 minutes or until *al dente*. Heat another large pan over a high heat. Add the clams and the wine, cover and cook over a high heat for 2–3 minutes until they have all just opened. (Discard any that stay closed.) Tip them into a colander set over a bowl to collect the clam juices.

Add all but the last tablespoon or two of the clam cooking liquor (which might be gritty) to the porcini sauce, return to the heat and simmer rapidly until it has reduced by half to a well-flavoured sauce.

Drain the pasta and return to the pan with the cooked clams, the porcini sauce and parsley and toss together well. Serve immediately.

WHILE TRAVELLING IN SICILY, Sardinia and Puglia I was struck by the large number of pasta dishes where some sort of brassica was among the ingredients: turnip tops (*cime de rape*), broccoli and, as in this case, cauliflower. Interestingly, contrary to what I generally prefer with brassicas, they always slightly over-cook the greens to produce a softer texture that partly thickens the rest of the sauce – it complements the pasta beautifully. It goes without saying that the anchovies in the sauce should be of very high quality. *Serves 4*

DITALI PASTA
WITH CAULIFLOWER, SAFFRON AND TOMATO CREAM SAUCE
SICILY

25 g anchovy fillets in olive oil, drained

5 tablespoons extra virgin olive oil

50 g fresh white breadcrumbs

1 large cauliflower, leaves and core removed, the rest broken into small florets (you will need about 750 g)

5 garlic cloves, finely chopped

1 medium-hot red chilli, seeded and finely chopped, or ½ teaspoon crushed dried chillies

3 tablespoons sun-dried tomato paste

A large pinch of saffron strands

450 g ditali or another small, tubular pasta

5 canned plum tomatoes, coarsely chopped (juice from the can reserved for another dish)

2 tablespoons double cream

2 tablespoons chopped flat-leaf parsley

Salt and freshly ground black pepper

Finely grated parmesan cheese, to serve

Put the anchovies into a small frying pan and leave over a low heat for 2–3 minutes until they have 'melted'. Set aside.

Heat 1 tablespoon of the olive oil in a large, deep frying pan, add the breadcrumbs and stir over a medium-low heat until crisp and golden. Season with a little salt and pepper and tip onto a plate lined with kitchen paper. Set aside.

In the same frying pan, heat the remaining oil, add the cauliflower florets and cook over a medium heat for 5 minutes without colouring, stirring now and then, until they start to soften. Add the garlic, chilli and some seasoning and cook for 1 more minute.

Mix the sun-dried tomato paste with 120 ml water, stir it into the cauliflower, cover and cook over a low heat for 15 minutes or until the cauliflower is just tender.

Meanwhile, cover the saffron with 50 ml warm water and leave it to soak. Bring 4.5 litres water to the boil in a large saucepan with 8 teaspoons salt. Add the pasta and cook for 9–10 minutes or until *al dente*.

Add the saffron water, tomatoes and anchovies to the cauliflower and season to taste. Increase the heat slightly and continue to cook uncovered, stirring now and then, until the cauliflower is very soft. Break up the florets into slightly smaller pieces with a wooden spoon if necessary, and then stir in the cream and parsley.

Drain the pasta well, return to the pan and add the sauce. Toss together well, spoon into warmed bowls and serve sprinkled with some parmesan cheese.

I LOVE OCCASIONS like this. We were in the north of Sardinia on our way from filming a Vermentino wine maker, Alberto Ragnedda, near Arzachena, to film cork-making at Calangianus, about 50 kilometres south. We love to follow our noses and stop somewhere half decent for lunch, but this day we seemed to be out of luck. I went into a bar in the tiny village of Sant'Antonio di Gallura to ask if they knew of anywhere we could eat. It looked a bit rough, with a jukebox in the corner, but a man behind the bar pointed to a closed door and said we could eat there if we liked. I opened the door, and there was a beautiful dining room filled with locals. The scent of pasta with tomato and meat sauce was almost too much to bear. I rushed out and grabbed everyone and we had the most memorable lunch, all of us filled with wonderment at our good fortune at finding perfection in the middle of nowhere. But that sums up the best of the Mediterranean: local enjoyment of good food is taken as read. I've based this dish on what I ate there. Just don't ask me for the name of the restaurant – go there and follow your nose. However, I do remember the wine was called Cannonau di Sardegna, a light and rather quaffable red. Gnocchetti sardi, also called malloreddus, is small, shell-shaped pasta, normally served in Sardinia with some sort of ragù, often made with game. I've added more fennel seeds, though these are often in their sausages anyway, and some dried porcini. I've also included a pinch of dried chilli, not uncommon in southern Italy. *Serves 4*

GNOCCHETTI SARDI
WITH MOUNTAIN SAUSAGE RAGU
SARDINIA

15 g dried porcini

3 tablespoons extra virgin olive oil

1 small onion, finely chopped

3 garlic cloves, thinly sliced

½ teaspoon crushed dried chillies

1 teaspoon fennel seeds, lightly crushed

350 g meaty pork sausages, skins removed
   and the meat crumbled into small pieces

120 ml dry white wine

400-g can chopped tomatoes

450 g gnocchetti sardi pasta

Salt and freshly ground black pepper

A little grated pecorino sardo maturo or
   parmesan cheese, to serve (optional)

Cover the porcini mushrooms with 100 ml boiling water and leave to soak for 30 minutes. Then drain, reserving the liquid, and finely chop.

Bring 4.5 litres water to the boil in a large saucepan with 8 teaspoons salt. Meanwhile, heat the olive oil in a medium-sized pan, add the onion, garlic, crushed dried chillies and fennel seeds and fry gently until lightly browned.

Add the sausagemeat and porcini and fry for 5 minutes. Add the wine and leave it to bubble down for 2 minutes, then add the tomatoes, mushroom-soaking liquor, ½ teaspoon salt and some pepper. Leave to simmer for 25–30 minutes until the sauce has reduced and thickened, then adjust the seasoning if necessary.

Add the pasta to the boiling water and cook for 9 minutes or until *al dente*. Drain, return to the pan and add the sausage ragù. Stir together well and serve sprinkled with a little grated cheese if you wish.

THIS COMES FROM CATANIA on the east coast of Sicily, a town with a black cathedral and a black lava elephant at the front of it. It's also the town where the driving is the most scary in the whole of Europe, but the food is wonderful, particularly this. The dish was apparently named after Bellini's opera, but it could also be referring to the use of the 'normal' ingredients of Sicily: aubergines, garlic, tomato, olive oil and basil. Either way you'd be hard pushed to find a better dish to satisfy a discerning vegetarian. *Serves 4*

PASTA ALLA NORMA:
PASTA WITH AUBERGINES, TOMATOES, CHILLI AND RICOTTA SALATA CHEESE
SICILY

500 g aubergines (about 2 large ones)

500 g small flavoursome tomatoes, or the very best canned plum tomatoes, such as San Marzano, drained

6 tablespoons extra virgin olive oil

400 g dried spaghetti

4 garlic cloves, crushed

¼ teaspoon crushed dried chillies

A large handful of fresh basil leaves, torn into small pieces

100 g finely grated ricotta salata or crumbled feta cheese

Salt and freshly ground black pepper

Top and tail the aubergines and cut them across into two, then each piece lengthways into sticks about the size of chips. Toss them with 1 teaspoon of salt, place them in colander set over a bowl and leave them for 30–40 minutes.

Meanwhile, squeeze fresh tomatoes, if using, over the sink to get rid of most of the juice. Coarsely chop the tomatoes, if large, and set aside. Bring 4.5 litres water to the boil in a large saucepan with 8 teaspoons salt.

Pat the aubergines dry with kitchen paper to remove the salt and juices. Heat 4 tablespoons of the oil in large frying pan, add half the aubergines and fry until lightly golden. Lift onto a plate lined with more kitchen paper and leave to drain while you cook the remainder. Allow the oil remaining in the frying pan to cool (if you were to add the garlic now, it would burn).

Drop the spaghetti into the boiling water and cook for 9 minutes or until *al dente*. Shortly before the pasta is ready, add the remaining olive oil and the garlic to the frying pan and return it to the heat. As soon as the garlic begins to gently sizzle, add the crushed chillies and the tomatoes and cook over a high heat for 2–3 minutes until they have broken down into a sauce. Season to taste with salt and pepper and stir in the aubergines.

Drain the pasta, add to the sauce with the basil and half the cheese and toss together well. Divide between warmed bowls, sprinkle with the remaining cheese and serve.

I HAVE MENTIONED the Tonnara di Bonagia just outside Trapani. The thing about the couscous we ate there was that it was so simple. Just an excellent seafood broth stirred into mounds of steamed couscous flavoured with bay and nutmeg. Indeed when David, the director, and I ate it, it came on a big dish as simply as that, but when we went back to film the cooking of it a couple of days later, we noticed that they served it up garnished with freshly cooked local prawns for a party of about twenty local bank managers and solicitors, and accompanied it with some of the broth heated up with quite a lot of chilli. *Serves 6*

SEAFOOD COUSCOUS
SICILY

2–3 tablespoons olive oil
24 large, raw, unpeeled prawns
Salt and freshly ground black pepper

For the stock
80 ml olive oil
1 large onion, sliced
4 garlic cloves, chopped
¼ teaspoon freshly grated nutmeg
500 ml tomato passata
½ teaspoon freshly ground white pepper
1.5 kg mixed fish such as gurnard, whiting,

grey mullet, conger eel, cut into thick
slices

For the couscous
5 tablespoons olive oil
3 fresh bay leaves
500 g quick-cook couscous
1 large onion, finely chopped
½ teaspoon freshly grated
nutmeg
2 tablespoons chopped flat-leaf parsley
1 teaspoon freshly ground white pepper

For the stock, heat the oil in a large pan over a medium heat. Add the onion and garlic and sweat gently for 5–6 minutes until soft. Add the nutmeg, passata, white pepper, 2 litres water and 2 teaspoons salt. Bring to the boil, add the fish and simmer, part-covered, for 2 hours. Strain the stock through a fine sieve into a clean pan, pressing out as much of the liquid as you can with the back of a ladle, and set aside. Discard what's left in the sieve.

For the couscous, preheat the oven to 150°C/Gas Mark 3. Bring 500 ml water, 2 tablespoons of the oil, the bay leaves and 1 teaspoon salt to the boil in a large pan. Stir in the couscous, cover and set aside for 2 minutes. Uncover, and fluff up into separate grains with a fork (or your fingers). Heat the remaining olive oil in a large flameproof casserole, add the onion and cook gently for 5–6 minutes until soft and very lightly golden. Add the couscous, nutmeg, parsley,

pepper and ½ teaspoon salt. Stir together well, cover and place in the oven for 15 minutes.

Shortly before serving, bring the seafood broth back up to the boil, then lower the heat and keep hot. Heat the 2–3 tablespoons olive oil in a frying pan. Season the prawns well with salt and pepper, add to the pan and fry for 2 minutes until lightly browned and cooked through.

Stir 450 ml of the hot broth through the couscous and spoon it onto 1 large serving dish or 6 warmed plates and scatter the prawns on top. Pour some more of the seafood broth into a jug and serve alongside the couscous.

NOTE: For the chilli broth, pour 175 ml of the broth into a small pan and add ½ teaspoon crushed dried chillies and 1 tablespoon olive oil. Heat for a few minutes, then pour into a bowl and serve.

ORZOTTO AI FRUTTI DI MARE:

PEARL BARLEY RISOTTO WITH LOBSTER AND MUSSELS

PUGLIA

I ATE THIS on the waterfront in Otranto in Puglia. I wasn't filled with confidence about a risotto made with pearl barley. It seemed a bit contrived, but I was wrong – it's just a local variation of risotto. The bite to pearl barley is pleasurable, as indeed it is in Irish stew. Here I've used the shell of a lobster to flavour the stock and then added the meat at the end, and the result is something quite special. By the way, the older pearl barley is, the longer it can take to cook. Be prepared for it to take anything up to an hour to become *al dente*. *Serves 4*

50 g butter

1 medium onion, finely chopped

2 garlic cloves, finely chopped

300 g pearl barley

150 ml dry white wine

20 mussels, cleaned

1 large vine tomato, skinned, seeded and diced

Chopped flat-leaf parsley, to garnish

Salt and freshly ground black pepper

For the Mediterranean seafood broth

1 x 450-g cooked lobster

4 tablespoons extra virgin olive oil

1 medium onion, roughly chopped

25 g garlic cloves, thinly sliced

1 fennel bulb, sliced

1 red pepper, seeded and roughly chopped

4 black olives, stones removed and roughly chopped

A large pinch of peperoncino or crushed dried chillies

120 ml dry white wine

1 kg inexpensive well-flavoured fish, such as gurnard, cut across into slices

A pinch of saffron strands

2 tablespoons tomato purée

For the broth, cut the lobster in half and remove the meat from the claws and the tail. Cut the tail meat across into slices, place in a bowl with the claw meat, cover and set aside. Cut up the lobster shells into chunky pieces. Heat the oil in a large pan, add the onions and garlic, and fry over a medium-high heat until lightly browned. Add the fennel, red pepper, black olives, peperoncino or crushed dried chillies and wine, and fry for a further 10 minutes. Add the lobster shells, gurnard, saffron, tomato purée and 2 litres water and leave to simmer gently, uncovered, for 45 minutes.

When the broth is ready, crush everything down into the stock with a potato masher to release as much flavour as possible from the ingredients. Then pass through a fine sieve into a clean pan, bring back to the boil and reduce to 1.2 litres. Add 1 teaspoon salt and keep hot.

For the orzotto, melt the butter in a medium-sized pan, add the onion and garlic and cook gently until soft but not browned. Add the pearl barley and cook for 2 minutes, stirring, then add the wine and simmer, stirring, until the wine has almost disappeared. Add a ladleful of the hot seafood stock and stir over a medium heat until it has been absorbed before adding another. Continue like this for about 40 minutes until the pearl barley is cooked but still a little *al dente*. You might not need to use all the stock.

As you come to add the last ladleful of stock, stir in the mussels, diced tomato and lobster meat and continue to cook for about 3 minutes until the mussels have opened and the lobster meat has heated through. Adjust the seasoning to taste and serve straight away in warmed bowls, sprinkled with a little chopped parsley.

ANY COMBINATION of chorizo and chickpeas is good for me, but with the addition of some good plum tomatoes and young spinach it makes for a very pleasing starter, tapas or side dish, particularly when the chickpeas are slow-cooked with a little cinnamon first and then gently stewed with the other ingredients. *Serves 6 as a starter or 12 as part of some mixed tapas*

CHICKPEA, CHORIZO, TOMATO AND SPINACH STEW
CATALONIA

350 g dried chickpeas, soaked overnight

1 small onion, quartered

1 celery stick, cut into 4 pieces

2 bay leaves

4 fresh thyme sprigs

7.5-cm piece cinnamon stick

3 tablespoons extra virgin olive oil

125 g shallots, thinly sliced

3 garlic cloves, finely chopped

100 g chorizo picante, thinly sliced

400 g can good quality plum tomatoes

150 g baby leaf spinach

Salt and freshly ground black pepper

Port de Soller, Mallorca

Drain the soaked chickpeas and put them into a pan with the onion, celery, bay leaves, thyme, cinnamon stick and enough water to cover by about 5 cm. Bring to the boil, lower the heat and leave them to simmer until the skins begin to crack and the peas are tender – about 40–45 minutes, adding 1 teaspoon salt 5 minutes before the end. Drain, reserving the cooking liquor, but discard the onion, celery, bay leaves, thyme and cinnamon stick.

In a large, deep frying pan or shallow casserole, heat the olive oil over a medium heat. Add the shallot, garlic and chorizo sausage and leave to cook gently, stirring occasionally, for 5 minutes. Add the tomatoes and cook for another 2–3 minutes, then add the chickpeas and 600 ml reserved cooking liquor and leave to simmer slowly for 45 minutes until almost all the liquid has gone.

Add the spinach and cook until just wilted down into the sauce, then season and serve.

THESE SHELLFISH AND RICE dishes from Spain are some of the nicest ways of eating seafood. They come in all forms, from a simple fisherman's *Arroz a la banda*, which is just shellfish stock and rice baked until crisp (and for which I did a recipe in *Rick Stein's Food Heroes, Another Helping*, page 70), to the mighty heights of a good paella. This dish from Andratx in Mallorca is bursting with flavour and really very easy to make. You can clearly see a link between these dishes and the jambalayas from the southern states of America. *Serves 6*

ARROZ A LA MARINERA:
RICE IN A PAELLA PAN WITH SQUID, PEPPERS AND SAFFRON
MALLORCA

3 medium-sized squid (about 1 kg),
    cleaned
3 tablespoons olive oil
6 garlic cloves, chopped
1 large onion, chopped
1 red pepper, seeded and chopped
1 green pepper, seeded and chopped
3 tomatoes, chopped
350 g paella rice, such as Mallorcan

bomba or Spanish arroz calasparra
1.2 litres *Mediterranean seafood broth*
    (see page 169), made with ½ teaspoon
    curry powder
A large handful of flat-leaf parsley leaves,
    roughly chopped
A large pinch of saffron stamens
Salt and freshly ground black pepper

Cut the squid in 3–4-cm pieces. Heat the oil in a shallow ovenproof frying pan or paella pan that's 30 cm in diameter, over a high heat. Add the garlic and squid, season with salt and pepper and fry for 2 minutes, stirring.

Push the squid to the outside edges of the pan, add the onion to the centre and fry for a minute or so, stirring, until slightly softened. Push the onion to the outside edges of the pan and add the red and green peppers – fry for another 2 minutes then push aside.

Add the tomato to the pan and fry for a couple of minutes. Stir in the rice and mix everything together. Add the stock, parsley and saffron and leave to simmer, without stirring, for about 20 minutes until most of the stock has been absorbed and the rice is tender but still *al dente*.

Meanwhile, preheat the oven to 230°C/Gas Mark 8 or as high as it will go. Transfer the pan to the hot oven and cook for 4 minutes to crisp up the top of the rice. Take the pan to the table and serve.

THIS CLASSIC SICILIAN RECIPE celebrates the wonderful anchovies we filmed being made in Sciacca by the family company of Agostino Recca. The difference between anchovies of this quality and the run-of-the-mill ones is enormous. These anchovies are sweet and succulent, but the other important ingredient in this dish is the tomato paste. It's called strattu, and is made by drying sieved tomato pulp and salt in the sun for a long time until it becomes dark red and clay-like. I've never found this in the UK and had only read about it, so when I finally got to La Vucciria market in Palermo, I made a beeline for a stall selling it from a vast bowl. It's so thick and stiff they merely wrap it up in paper. *Serves 4*

SPAGHETTINI
WITH ANCHOVIES, PARSLEY AND CRISP BREADCRUMBS
SICILY

For the sauce

2 tablespoons strattu (see above) or tomato purée
5 tablespoons olive oil
3 garlic cloves, finely chopped
10 anchovy fillets in olive oil, drained
400 g dried spaghettini
Salt and freshly ground black pepper

For the breadcrumbs

4 fat garlic cloves, peeled
6 tablespoons extra virgin olive oil
225 g white breadcrumbs, made from day-old white bread
8 anchovy fillets in olive oil, drained
4 tablespoons chopped flat-leaf parsley

Bring 4.5 litres water to the boil in a large saucepan with 8 teaspoons salt. For the breadcrumbs, lightly crush the garlic under the blade of a large knife. Put the crushed cloves into a large frying pan with 5 tablespoons of the oil and place the pan over a medium heat. Fry the garlic until it just starts to colour, then remove and discard. Add the breadcrumbs to the oil and fry over a medium heat, stirring constantly, for about 5 minutes until crisp and golden. Spoon onto a plate and wipe the pan clean. Chop the anchovy fillets. Add the remaining tablespoon of oil to the pan, add the chopped anchovy and cook over a low heat, breaking them up a little with a wooden spoon, until they have dissolved into the oil. Return the breadcrumbs to the pan with the parsley and a little seasoning and stir together well. Set aside and keep warm.

For the sauce, mix the strattu or tomato purée with 2 tablespoons hot water until smooth. Put the oil and garlic into another frying pan and place over a medium heat. As soon as the garlic begins to sizzle, add the tomato paste, anchovies and 175 ml water and leave to simmer gently for 10 minutes.

Meanwhile, drop the spaghettini into the pan of boiling water and cook for 5–6 minutes or until *al dente*. Drain well, return to the pan, add the sauce and toss together well. Divide the spaghettini between 4 warmed serving bowls and sprinkle with some of the anchovy bread-crumbs. Serve the rest of the breadcrumbs separately.

I HAVE ALREADY enthused about the kebab restaurant Imam Cagdas in Gaziantep (see page 144). When the owner, Burhan, suggested we film his wife, Gulsen, cooking a bulgar wheat pilaf, I was enthusiastic. They took us to one of the oldest houses in the town, which they were in the process of restoring and turning into a cookery school, but when we saw the kitchen, I thought we were in for what we call in the trade 'a strawberry filter'. This is when you pretend to film but don't actually use any tape. Gulsen seemed rather too well turned out to do any serious cooking, and the kitchen looked like a museum piece. But not only was she a good cook, she also explained clearly what she was doing. For instance, she pointed out her mixing of bulgar wheat with what they call frik to give the pilaf a uniquely smoky, earthy taste. Frik is made from immature green wheat. They set the corn ears on fire to burn off the chaff, and then use the moist green kernels. Even without the frik, the recipe is worth making. Serve with the Turkish mixed leaf salad on page 43. *Serves 6–8*

BULGAR WHEAT PILAF
WITH LAMB, ALMONDS AND PISTACHIO NUTS
TURKEY

500 g boneless leg of lamb

5 tablespoons olive oil

4 tablespoons tomato purée

2 onions, peeled

2 red peppers, stalk and seeds removed, cut into small chunks

4 garlic cloves, chopped

2 tablespoons *Turkish red pepper paste* (see page 209)

500 g coarse bulgar wheat

125 g *Clarified butter* (see page 210)

1 tablespoon Aleppo pepper

150 g blanched almonds

150 g shelled pistachio nuts

4 large mint sprigs, to garnish

Salt and freshly ground black pepper

Trim excess fat from the lamb and cut into 5-cm pieces. Heat 2 tablespoons of the olive oil in a medium-sized saucepan. Add the lamb and fry until nicely browned all over and all the juices from the meat have evaporated. Add 2 tablespoons of the tomato purée and fry for 1–2 minutes, then add 1 whole onion, 1 teaspoon salt and 2 litres water. Bring to the boil and leave to simmer gently for 1¼ hours, until the meat is very tender. Lift out and discard the onion. Strain the stock into a jug and, if it measures more than 1 litre, return to another pan and simmer rapidly until reduced to the required amount. Cover both the meat and stock and set to one side.

Finely chop the remaining onion. Heat the remaining olive oil in a flameproof casserole. Add the onion and red pepper chunks and fry until both are soft and lightly browned. Add the garlic and fry for 1 minute, then add the remaining tomato purée, the Turkish red pepper paste and the reserved lamb stock. Bring to the boil and stir in the bulgar wheat and 1 teaspoon freshly ground black pepper. Cover and leave to cook undisturbed over a low heat for

15 minutes, or until all the liquid has been absorbed and the bulgar is tender. Turn off the heat, uncover briefly, lay a couple of sheets of kitchen paper over the top of the pilaf and replace the lid. Leave to rest for 5 minutes – this will absorb any excess moisture.

Now heat 50 g of the clarified butter in a small pan. Add the Aleppo pepper and another teaspoon of black pepper and sizzle for a few seconds, then remove from the heat. Uncover the pilaf, remove the paper and fluff up the grains of bulgar with a fork. Drizzle over the spicy butter and stir once or twice through the mixture until the bulgar glistens, then cover again and leave for a further 5 minutes.

Meanwhile, divide the remaining clarified butter between 2 small pans and warm over a medium heat. Add the blanched almonds to one pan and the pistachios to the other, and fry gently for 2–3 minutes until the nuts are lightly golden. Remove with a slotted spoon and drain separately on kitchen paper. Reheat the cooked lamb at the same time. Remove everything from the heat.

Spoon the bulgar pilaf onto a warmed oval serving dish and arrange the lamb pieces on top. Spoon the fried almonds around the edge of the pilaf and sprinkle the pistachios down the centre. Garnish with the mint sprigs and serve straight away.

THIS WAS A RATHER incidental dish from a trip to the Caffè Spinnato in the centre of Palermo. We had been told that this was the place where the great, the good and the powerful meet in that fabulous city, and so it proved to be. It was full of expensively suited men wearing dark glasses and kissing each other ostentatiously on the cheek. I was much impressed, and almost distracted from noticing how exquisite this simple pasta dish was, which used the special capers from the island of Pantelleria. *Serves 4*

PASTA WITH TOMATOES, CAPERS AND MINT
SICILY

400 g dried spaghetti

500 g small vine or cherry tomatoes

4 tablespoons extra virgin olive oil

2 fat garlic cloves, peeled and
　lightly flattened under the blade
　of a knife

A large pinch of crushed dried
　chillies

1 tablespoon small salted capers,
　rinsed and drained

10 g mint leaves, roughly chopped

Salt and freshly ground black
　pepper

Bring 4.5 litres water to the boil in a large saucepan with 8 teaspoons salt. Add the pasta and cook for 9 minutes or until *al dente*.

Meanwhile, skin the tomatoes (by immersing briefly in hot water then taking the skins off with your hands), squeeze them over the sink to rid of their seeds, then roughly chop.

Heat the olive oil in a large, deep frying pan with the garlic cloves and fry gently until they begin to colour. Remove and discard the garlic cloves. Add the crushed dried chillies and tomatoes to the pan and fry for 30 seconds to 1 minute until they have just started to release their juices. Add the capers and mint, and season to taste with salt and pepper.

Drain the spaghetti, add to the pan and toss well. Divide between warmed bowls and serve.

GIGANDES PLAKI:
LARGE WHITE BUTTER BEANS
IN TOMATO SAUCE

CORFU

ALTHOUGH *plaki* means oven-baked in Greek, I've cooked these beans on the top of the stove because it's a bit quicker and I think it's easier to keep an eye on things. The first time I arrived in Greece was with a bit of a hangover on the Brindisi to Igoumenitsa ferry. We stopped off at a taverna in the mountains about 20 miles out of town. I was with my ex-wife, Jill, then my girlfriend, and my brother and a friend called John Thompson. They both knew the score in Greece, so we walked straight through to the kitchen and lifted the lid of the nearest gigantic pan, only to see half a dozen goat's heads simmering in a stew. I must say, with my hangover, I thought I was never going to find anything to eat if it was all going to be like this. Then I saw a much smaller pot filled with giant butter beans in tomato sauce and I thought, 'Ah, local baked beans. I'm going to be OK.' And indeed they were fantastic and I've loved them ever since. *Serves 6 as a side dish or 12 as part of a mixed mezze*

500 g large butter beans, such as Spanish Judión beans, soaked overnight
250 ml olive oil
1 medium onion, chopped
3 garlic cloves, finely chopped
1 kg ripe flavoursome tomatoes, skinned and chopped, or 2 x 400-g cans chopped tomatoes
1 tablespoon tomato purée
1 teaspoon sweet paprika
A good pinch of ground allspice
2 fresh bay leaves
1 tablespoon chopped dill
2 tablespoons chopped flat-leaf parsley
Salt and freshly ground black pepper

Drain and rinse the beans and put them into a saucepan with enough cold water to cover by about 5 cm. Bring to the boil, reduce the heat to low and leave to simmer gently until soft – about 45–50 minutes, but this will depend on the age of the beans. Do watch them, as they can disintegrate very quickly once soft.

Meanwhile, heat 150 ml of the olive oil in a medium-sized pan, add the onion and garlic and cook gently until soft but not browned. Add the tomatoes, tomato purée, paprika, allspice and bay leaves and simmer for about 25 minutes, until the sauce has thickened and some of the oil has risen to the surface. Remove and discard the bay leaves, transfer to a food processor and blend to a smooth sauce. Return to the pan and season to taste with salt and pepper.

Drain the beans, reserving the cooking liquor, and add the beans to the sauce with 150 ml cooking liquor and 2 teaspoons salt or to taste. Simmer for another 30 minutes. Stir in the remaining olive oil, chopped dill and parsley and serve at room temperature.

WHAT A WORK OF ART the dried broad bean is. Of all pulses I think it has the most profound flavour. Every time I came across dishes using broad beans, I find myself thinking I could probably survive on them and not a lot else, especially served up in the myriad ways they are in the Mediterranean. This is a simple soup, a speciality of Chefchaouen, made with broad beans, water, garlic, olive oil, salt and cumin. It is served with the, to me, essential accompaniment of hot paprika and lemon. You can also find it served up as a thicker purée, again with oil and cumin and some fresh flatbread for dipping. Other additions for sprinkling on this warming, filling soup are chopped mint or thyme, or zahtar. *Serves 4*

BESSARA: DRIED BROAD BEAN SOUP WITH CUMIN, OLIVE OIL AND HOT PAPRIKA
MOROCCO

500 g dried shelled and split broad beans, soaked overnight	**Salt and freshly ground black pepper**	**Freshly ground cumin**
		Hot paprika
	To serve	**Lemon wedges**
6 garlic cloves, peeled	**Olive oil**	**Fresh wholemeal bread**

Drain and rinse the soaked broad beans and put them into a pan with 2.5 litres water. Bring to the boil over a medium heat, skimming off the foam as it rises to the surface. Add the garlic, lower the heat, part-cover and leave to cook for 1 hour until the beans are very soft and starting to disintegrate. Season with 2 teaspoons salt, remove from the heat and leave to cool slightly.

Blend the mixture in batches until smooth and creamy. Pass through a sieve, if you wish, back into a clean pan, adjust the seasoning if necessary and reheat gently, adding a little extra water if the soup is too thick.

Ladle the soup into warmed bowls and drizzle with a generous amount of olive oil, then sprinkle with plenty of freshly ground cumin. Serve with a bowl of hot paprika for sprinkling, and lemon wedges, which people can add to their own taste. Eat with plenty of wholemeal bread.

VARIATION

DRIED BROAD BEAN DIP
Simmer the soaked beans and garlic in 1 litre water for 30 minutes until the liquid has disappeared and the beans are soft and falling apart. Tip into a food processor, add 1 teaspoon salt and blend into a smooth purée. Stir in 2 tablespoons extra virgin olive oil and 2–3 tablespoons water to give a slightly looser purée. Adjust the seasoning to taste and spoon into a shallow serving dish. Serve still warm, sprinkled with olive oil, ground cumin and hot paprika, with lemon wedges and some flatbread or pitta bread.

SWEET THINGS: ICES

FRUITS

CAKES

STICKY PASTRIES

A BITE OF SOMETHING RICH AND
SWEET OR REFRESHING AND COLD
TO FINISH OFF A MEDITERRANEAN FEAST

Tangier, Morocco

THERE ARE SOME who say that crème brûlée is derived from crema catalana, and indeed both are made in a similar way – a set custard is sprinkled with sugar and caramelized – but I think it would be hard to establish which came first. In Barcelona, the cream is flavoured with orange and cinnamon, and you can still buy the hot irons with which the sugar is burnt on top. These days most people use a blowtorch, though I think if you've got a good hot overhead grill, you get a better flavour. *Serves 4*

CREMA CATALANA:
CATALAN CREME BRULEE
CATALONIA

300 ml single cream
300 ml full-cream milk
Finely grated zest ½ orange
Finely grated zest ½ large lemon
7.5-cm piece cinnamon stick, broken in half
4 large egg yolks
75 g caster sugar, plus 4 tablespoons
2 tablespoons cornflour

Bring the cream, milk, orange zest, lemon zest and the cinnamon stick halves to the boil in a non-stick pan. Set aside for 1 hour for the milk to become infused with the flavourings.

Put the egg yolks into a bowl, add the 75 g sugar and beat with a hand-held electric mixer until pale and creamy. Beat in the cornflour.

Bring the milk back to the boil and strain into a jug. Mix a few tablespoons into the egg yolk mixture to loosen it slightly, then stir in the remainder.

Pour the mixture back into the pan and cook over a low heat for 4–5 minutes, stirring all the time, until the mixture has thickened and coats the back of the wooden spoon. But don't let the mixture boil.

Pour the mixture into 4 wide shallow dishes (terracotta if possible), measuring about 12 cm across. Leave to cool, then chill for 4–6 hours, or overnight.

Shortly before serving, sprinkle the surface of each custard with 1 tablespoon of the remaining sugar and caramelize under a hot grill or with a blowtorch. Serve immediately – the sugar will only stay hard for about 30 minutes.

SEMI-FREDDO means half frozen, which is how you should serve up this ice cream. That is, you freeze it and then let it soften a little before dishing it up. It seems to me to be one of the best Italian sweets going. It's a simple ice-cream mixture into which you can fold whatever you like: crushed amaretti biscuits, marsala, limoncello, chopped chocolate. Here I've used the totally delicious, crumbly almond nougat from Sardinia, called *torrone*. If you bash that up with a rolling pin, fold it into your mixture and freeze it, then serve it with raspberries and brandy snaps, you have the sort of pudding that everybody loves and will want more of. This is a great dish to serve up at a summer party. For a smaller amount, halve the recipe. *Serves 10–12*

SEMI-FREDDO:
ALMOND NOUGAT WITH RASPBERRIES AND ORANGE BRANDY SNAPS
SARDINIA

400 g crunchy-style torrone (almond nougat)
1 vanilla pod
4 large eggs, separated
50 g caster sugar
500 ml double cream

A small pinch of salt
2 tablespoons clear honey

For the orange brandy snaps
75 g unsalted butter
75 g caster sugar
75 g golden syrup

75 g plain flour
¾ teaspoon finely grated orange zest
1½ teaspoons orange juice
Fresh raspberries, to serve

Put the nougat into a plastic bag and smash it up into tiny pieces with a rolling pin. Don't do this too far in advance or it will get sticky.

Slit open the vanilla pod lengthways and scrape out the seeds. Reserve the pod for another dish or store it in a jar of sugar. Using an electric whisk, beat the egg yolks, sugar and vanilla seeds in a bowl for 4–5 minutes until they are thick and pale.

In another large bowl, whip the cream into soft peaks. In a third bowl whisk the egg whites with the salt into stiff peaks. Gently fold the whipped cream, nougat and honey into the egg yolk mixture, followed by the egg whites, and then spoon it into a shallow serving dish. You want the mixture to be about 7.5 cm deep. Cover with clingfilm and freeze it overnight.

For the brandy snaps, preheat the oven to 180°C/Gas Mark 4. Line a baking sheet with non-stick baking paper. Put the butter, sugar and golden syrup into a small pan and heat gently until the sugar has dissolved and the mixture is smooth. Remove from the heat and stir in the flour, orange zest and juice. Place 6 level teaspoons of the mixture, 8 cm apart, onto the prepared baking sheet and bake for 7 minutes until deeply golden. Remove from the oven and leave for 1 minute to cool slightly. Then lift them off, one at a time, with a palette knife and curl them over a roll of clingfilm or foil or a rolling pin into tuile shapes. Leave to go cold and harden. If they harden too much before you have time to shape them, just put them briefly back in the oven until soft again. Repeat with the remaining mixture and store in an airtight tin until needed.

To serve, remove the ice cream from the freezer and allow it to thaw slightly until *semi-freddo*, half frozen. Serve in scoops with some raspberries and the brandy snaps.

I HAVE ALREADY MENTIONED the impressive furore of activity at Imam Cagdas, the kebab restaurant in Gaziantep, and this was especially so on the first floor where they were making baklava. There must have been 50 or 60 people preparing the paper-thin pastry and the bright green pistachios, building up the trays of baklava and baking them in the huge, wood-fired ovens. But only two people, Burhan Cagdas's ageing father and one other, were allowed to apply the boiling hot syrup after baking, which had to be at just the right temperature and consistency. There was so much flour in the air where the pastries were being assembled that everyone seemed to be working in a dream-like haze. The most distinctive elements, apart from the perfect pastry, were the vibrantly green pistachios, harvested when young, and the butter made from ewe's milk. This is their recipe and is still very good even when made with ordinary butter and pistachios, and is just perfect with a cup of strong black coffee – Turkish, of course. *Makes about 20 pieces*

BAKLAVA

TURKEY

500 g filo pastry sheets

150 g *Clarified butter* (see page 210), warmed

250 g shelled pistachio nuts, finely chopped by hand

For the pastry cream

300 ml milk

40 g semolina

For the syrup

600 g granulated sugar

1 teaspoon lemon juice

First make the pastry cream. Put the milk and semolina into a small, non-stick pan and slowly bring to the boil, stirring. Simmer for 1 minute, then transfer the mixture to a bowl, press a sheet of clingfilm onto the surface to prevent it from forming a skin and leave to go cold.

Preheat the oven to 160°C/Gas Mark 3. Cut down the filo pastry sheets if necessary so they will line a 20 x 30-cm shallow, rectangular, non-stick baking tin. Brush the base and sides of the tin with some of the clarified butter, then line the base with 15 single layers of pastry, brushing each one lightly with butter before adding the next. Don't butter the last sheet of pastry.

Mix the pastry cream until smooth, loosening it slightly with a little milk if it seems stiff, then spread it evenly over the top of the pastry. Sprinkle over the chopped pistachios in an even layer. Cover the top of the baklava with another 15 layers of filo pastry, lightly brushing with butter between each layer.

Using a large, very sharp knife, cut the baklava into portion-sized pieces – make 3 evenly spaced cuts lengthways down the tin and then cut across at an angle to make small, diamond-shaped pieces. Drizzle over any remaining butter. Bake the baklava for 1 hour until crisp and richly golden.

Meanwhile, for the sugar syrup, put the sugar and 350 ml water into a pan and leave over a low heat until the sugar has completely dissolved and the mixture is clear. Then bring to the boil and simmer vigorously until it reaches 107–108°C, the 'thread' stage – you will need a sugar thermometer to check. Add the lemon juice to the syrup and set aside.

A minute or two before the baklava is ready to come out of the oven, bring the sugar syrup back up to the boil. Remove the baklava from the oven, quickly and carefully run a knife along the cuts to check the pieces are all separate, then immediately pour over the hot syrup. This will look like a large amount, but it will gradually be absorbed by the pastry as it cools. Leave the baklava to go cold, then carefully remove from the tin to serve.

IT IS CURIOUS the way inconsequential events stay with you. Just above Trapani, in the little village of Erice, is a beautiful viewpoint. On a good day the views across to Egadi islands are spectacular, as is the panorama of Trapani itself. But I think, in fact I know, that we were all guilty of having one too many beers the night before, and the zigzagging of the road up to the top was torturous. No one seemed to notice that the weather was distinctly grey before we set off, and when we got there, there was no view worth recording, or at least nothing we couldn't just as easily have seen at sea level. However, before returning we sat down and ordered affogatos all round, and then it all seemed worthwhile. Just one word of warning. This has to be made with proper, strong espresso, so unless you have a machine, save the pleasure for the next time you are in an Italian restaurant. All other types of coffee are too watery and lack the necessary intensity of flavour. *Serves 4*

AFFOGATO: VANILLA ICE CREAM WITH HOT ESPRESSO, WALNUT LIQUEUR AND GRATED CHOCOLATE
SICILY

4 x 30-ml shots (8 tablespoons) freshly
    made espresso coffee

4 tablespoons walnut or hazelnut liqueur

4 teaspoons finely grated plain chocolate

For the vanilla ice cream

2 vanilla pods

500 ml full-cream milk

6 egg yolks

200 g caster sugar

500 ml single or double cream

1 teaspoon vanilla extract

For the vanilla ice cream, slit open the vanilla pods and scrape out the seeds with the tip of a knife. Put the milk and vanilla pods and seeds into a non-stick pan and bring to the boil, then remove from heat and set aside for 30 minutes to infuse the milk with the flavour of the vanilla.

Put the egg yolks and caster sugar into a large bowl and, using an electric whisk, whisk for 3 minutes until pale and mousse-like. Bring the milk back to the boil, strain onto the egg yolk mixture and stir until well combined. Return to the pan and cook over a low heat, stirring, for 3–4 minutes until the mixture lightly coats the back of a wooden spoon, but do not let the mixture boil or it will curdle. Remove from the heat and set aside to cool slightly, then stir in the cream and vanilla extract. Chill until cold, then churn in an ice-cream maker until smooth. Transfer to a plastic container, cover and freeze until required.

Just before serving, make 4 shots of strong espresso coffee. Drop 2 scoops of vanilla ice cream into each of 4 stemmed glasses and pour over the steaming hot coffee (2 tablespoons per glass) and then the liqueur. Sprinkle the ice cream with the chocolate and serve straight away.

THE FLOWER WATERS of Morocco are a good enough reason in themselves to go there. In Fes I found that you buy them from small perfume shops in the souks rather than food shops. Make sure you don't buy the concentrated version, which is also sold there, but as a perfume. And the oranges from Morocco are legendary in themselves. They are almost bursting with sweet juice, pleasingly balanced with acidity. I love these simple fruit dishes. This one is finished with a pinch of freshly ground cinnamon and a scattering of pomegranate seeds. *Serves 4*

MOROCCAN ORANGE SALAD
WITH CINNAMON, ORANGE FLOWER WATER AND POMEGRANATE SEEDS
MOROCCO

6 large juicy oranges

2 tablespoons icing sugar

1 tablespoon orange flower water

2.5-cm piece cinnamon stick

Seeds from ½ pomegranate

Slice the top and bottom off each orange and stand each one on a chopping board. Cutting from the top down to the bottom, carefully slice away all the skin and white pith. Then turn each orange on its side and cut the fruit across into thin slices.

Overlap the orange slices over the base of a wide, shallow plate and sprinkle with the icing sugar and orange flower water. Cover and set aside in the fridge for 1 hour.

Shortly before serving, put the piece of cinnamon stick into a spice grinder and grind to a slightly coarse powder. Sprinkle lightly over the oranges with the pomegranate seeds and serve.

Meknes, Morocco

CLEMENTINE AND CAMPARI SORBET

SICILY

75 g liquid glucose

200 g caster sugar

120 ml water

600 ml freshly squeezed
   clementine juice

Juice 2 large lemons

5 tablespoons Campari

Put the liquid glucose, sugar and water into a pan and slowly bring to the boil, stirring occasionally to dissolve the sugar. Remove from the heat and leave to cool.

Stir in the orange juice, lemon juice and Campari and strain into a bowl. Cover and chill for at least 2 hours. Churn in an ice-cream maker, then transfer to a shallow plastic container and freeze until required. Serve in scoops in small glasses.

AURELIO LUCATA is famous for his granita al limone, served from his little bar on the quayside in Sciacca on the south coast of Sicily. He looks a bit like Lee J. Cobb and boasts that his granita has a star in the Michelin guide. Actually it's mentioned in the Michelin green tourist guide, but it's bloody good granita, especially on a 40°C summer's day. I recall having three, one after the other, and thinking: 'I'm never going to stop eating these, ever.' The secret, he says, to their special fragrance is to use slightly green lemons. They were indeed a little under-ripe and a little misshapen in a thoroughly appetizing way. As he explained with great pride, the only ingredients are lemon juice, sugar and water, and in his case quite the oldest Capigini ice-cream maker I've ever seen, where the tinning in the bowl was worn through to the brass below. I had always been led to believe that granita was a flaky water ice, rather than this more sorbet-like creation, but who am I to argue with a master of his art such as Aurelio? *Serves 6–8*

GRANITA AL LIMONE:
SICILIAN LEMON GRANITA
SICILY

275 g granulated sugar

600 ml water

300 ml lemon juice (approximately 6
  juicy lemons), any stray pips removed

Bring the sugar and water to the boil in a pan and simmer for 5 minutes. Remove from the heat and leave to cool, then stir in the lemon juice, tasting the mixture to make sure you have the right degree of acidity. Churn in an ice-cream maker until smooth, then transfer to a plastic box, seal and store in the freezer until needed.

VARIATIONS

SEVILLE ORANGE GRANITA

Simply replace the lemon juice with Seville orange or blood orange juice.

THIS DELIGHTFUL CAKE is from Mallorca where almond trees grow in abundance. I love coming across something quite perfect like this rather unexpectedly. We were in an excellent tapas bar in Palma called Piensa en Verde and the waiter dropped a couple of pieces of this cake on our table for us to try, together with its accompanying almond ice cream. Unlike other types of ice cream, this is more like a sorbet, as it contains no cream or milk, and it seems to me to be the epitome of elegance, light and refreshing. The sort of thing you like to eat on a warm Spanish evening: a slice of cake, a dollop of ice cream and an espresso, watching what the Italians call *la passeggiata* – those elegant girls in their tight dresses and designer sunglasses leaving behind them maybe a trace of Maja soap in the air.
Makes 1 x 23-cm cake, to serve about 8

ALMOND CAKE
WITH ALMOND ICE CREAM
MALLORCA

For the almond ice cream

250 g blanched almonds

1 litre water

300 g caster sugar

Finely grated zest 1 lemon

5-cm piece cinnamon stick

For the almond cake

200 g blanched almonds

5 large eggs, separated

200 g caster sugar

Finely grated zest ½ lemon

½ teaspoon ground cinnamon

butter for greasing the tin

icing sugar for dusting (optional)

For the ice cream, put the almonds into a food processor and grind them to a fine powder. Put the water, almonds, sugar, lemon zest and cinnamon stick into a saucepan and bring very slowly to the boil, stirring frequently. As soon as the mixture comes to the boil, remove the pan from the heat and leave it to cool. Remove the cinnamon stick and churn in an ice-cream maker until smooth. Transfer to a plastic container, cover and freeze for at least 6 hours or until firm.

For the cake, preheat the oven to 170°C/Gas Mark 3. Grease a 23-cm round cake tin with butter and dust it out with flour. Put the almonds into a food processor and grind them to a very fine powder.

Using an electric whisk, beat the egg yolks and sugar together in a bowl for 4–5 minutes until pale and creamy. Fold in the almonds, lemon zest and cinnamon. The mixture will be quite stiff at this point.

Clean the beaters of the whisk, then use to beat the egg whites in a large clean bowl until they form soft peaks. Add 2 large spoonfuls of the egg whites to the mixture to loosen it slightly, then gently fold in the remainder. Pour the mixture into the prepared tin and bake for 40 minutes until a skewer, pushed into the centre of the cake, comes away clean.

Leave the cake to cool in the tin, then turn out and dust with icing sugar if you wish. Serve cut into wedges with a scoop or two of the almond ice cream.

UNLIKE TIRAMISU, which I always think is a bit heavy after a typically pasta-laden Italian meal, zabaglione is light and frivolous. When I was little my parents used to take me and my brothers and sisters to a restaurant in Soho called the Venezia, and the two dishes that I never tired of – and never will – were cannelloni and zabaglione. This version of zabaglione is made with red wine, a soft, earthy, deep red Primitivo from Puglia. For a traditional version, replace the red wine reduction with 120 ml Sicilian marsala. *Serves 4*

ZABAGLIONE:
RED WINE ZABAGLIONE
SICILY

250 ml Primitivo wine
100 g caster sugar
4 egg yolks

Savoiardi biscuits (see page 207), to serve

Put the Primitivo wine into a pan and simmer gently until reduced by half. Leave to cool then stir in 50 g of the sugar.

Put the egg yolks and the rest of the sugar into a heatproof glass bowl and beat with an electric whisk for about 5 minutes until thick and pale yellow.

Place the bowl over a pan of barely simmering water and continue to whisk for another 12–15 minutes, gradually drizzling in the red wine syrup, until the mixture almost triples in volume and is light and foamy and holding soft peaks. Take care not to get the mixture too hot or it will start to cook round the edges of the bowl and lose volume. Spoon into 4 tall glasses or bowls and serve warm with the savoiardi biscuits.

YOU MAY THINK the idea of strawberries immersed in red wine is bizarre, but these two ingredients have an almost symbiotic relationship. The strawberries bring out the soft mineral-like qualities of a wine like Primitivo, and the wine makes the strawberries taste deliciously crisp and astringently sweet. In addition, the vanilla will make the red wine taste like a grand cru. However, don't leave them to macerate for more than an hour, or the vanilla will dominate. I'm always looking for sweets that are light and simple, like this. *Serves 4*

STRAWBERRIES
IN PRIMITIVO WITH VANILLA
PUGLIA

500 g small, ripe strawberries

100 g caster sugar

500 ml soft fruity red wine, such as
    a Primitivo or Merlot

2 teaspoons lemon juice

1 vanilla pod, split open lengthways

Hull the strawberries and put them into a glass bowl with the sugar, red wine, lemon juice and vanilla pod. Mix together well, cover and chill for 1 hour. Serve them cold with some lightly whipped cream.

AMONG MY MEMORIES of driving by Land Rover to Greece in the early 1970s was the delicious yogurt there. In those days yogurt in Britain was thickened with what I now think was probably wheat starch. In Greece the ewe's milk yogurt was sold in little china dishes and had a thick top layer over which you drizzled honey, and it was a delight. A very close contender were the rice puddings, served in similar dishes. I used to love rice pudding at school, and I found these just as good. Thick and rich, and you could always taste the grains of rice in them, sometimes flavoured with lemon zest, other times with rose water. I remember one particularly hungover morning in Matala, the village on the south coast of Crete made famous by Joni Mitchell in the song 'Carey'. Are they still playing that scratchy rock 'n' roll on the BAL-AMi jukebox in the Mermaid café, I wonder? Well, that morning I blearily asked if they had giaourti or rizogalo. 'Ne,' they said, so I got up, muttering, 'Oh well, no yogurt or rice pudding today, I suppose,' and walked to the café next door. Needless to say they looked a bit perplexed. *Serves 4*

RIZOGALO: GREEK RICE PUDDING WITH LEMON AND CINNAMON

CORFU

150 g short-grain pudding rice
600 ml full-cream milk
Finely grated zest of ½ lemon or
  2 teaspoons rose water
2 teaspoons cornflour
75 g caster sugar
2 medium egg yolks
Ground cinnamon, for dusting

Place the rice in a pan with 300 ml water and simmer over a low heat for 8–10 minutes until most of the water has been absorbed.

Add all but 2 tablespoons of the milk and the lemon zest if using, and continue to simmer, part covered, for about 20 minutes, stirring every now and then, until the mixture is thick and creamy and the rice is just tender.

Mix the cornflour with the remaining milk and add to the rice with the sugar and the rose water if using. Simmer for another 3–4 minutes. Remove from the heat and leave to cool slightly.

Lightly beat the egg yolks, stir them into the rice slowly and then return the pan to a gentle heat and cook for about 30 seconds until thickened. Be careful not to get the mixture too hot or the eggs will scramble.

Spoon the mixture immediately into 4 small, shallow bowls and leave to cool. Sprinkle lightly with cinnamon and serve at room temperature.

I LIKE DOING a bit of business when I'm filming. Having met the Ravidà family and tasted their deliciously peppery olive oil, I now buy it for the Seafood Restaurant. It's poured into little bowls in which you can dunk your *pain au levain* as soon as you sit down. Natalia cooked half a dozen dishes for me at their farm near Menfi and they were all delicious, but sadly most of them you wouldn't be able to cook over here because getting the right ingredients is difficult. However, this tart, which I think is her mother's recipe, is superb, and is based on a recipe from her new book, *Seasons of Sicily*. I love the way the Sicilians use ricotta in their tarts and cakes. I'd love to do a recipe for cassata siciliana but it is too complicated for the average cook, including me, so at least this one gives you an idea of what the best Sicilian pastries are all about. *Serves 6–8*

NATALIA'S CHOCOLATE AND RICOTTA TART
SICILY

For the pastry case

250 g plain flour

65g caster sugar

A pinch of salt

100 g chilled lightly salted butter, cut into small pieces, plus extra for greasing

1 medium egg

1 medium egg yolk

1 tablespoon marsala

For the filling

750 g fresh ricotta cheese

125 g caster sugar

1 teaspoon vanilla extract

A pinch of salt

100 g good quality plain chocolate, finely chopped

½ teaspoon icing sugar

½ teaspoon cocoa powder

If your ricotta cheese is from a tub, tip it into a sieve set over a bowl, cover with clingfilm and leave in the fridge overnight to drain.

The next day, make the pastry. Sift the flour into a food processor, add the sugar and salt and chilled butter and process briefly until the mixture resembles fine breadcrumbs. Lightly beat the egg with the egg yolk and marsala. With the machine still running, gradually add the egg mixture to the bowl and process for a few seconds until the mixture just starts to come together. Tip out onto a lightly floured surface and knead briefly until smooth. Roll out thinly on a lightly floured surface and use to line a greased, loose-bottomed flan tin that is 4 cm deep and 23 cm across the base. Chill for 20 minutes. Meanwhile, preheat the oven to 200°C/Gas Mark 6.

Line the pastry case with a sheet of crumpled greaseproof paper and a thin layer of baking beans and bake for 15 minutes. Remove the paper and beans and return to the oven for 5 minutes. Remove, set to one side and lower the oven temperature to 180°C/Gas Mark 4.

For the filling, put the ricotta cheese into a clean bowl, add the sugar and beat together well until smooth. Stir in the vanilla extract, followed by the salt and the chopped chocolate. Spoon the mixture into the pastry case and spread out evenly with the back of a knife.

Bake the tart for 45 minutes until the edges of the pastry case are biscuit-coloured. Remove and leave to cool. Then remove from the tin and dust with the icing sugar and cocoa powder just before serving.

IN THE MID-SIXTIES I spent about a week in a youth hostel in Seville just by the railway station. I shared a room with a Swedish chap called Jonas. He had the best pair of worn patched Levi's I'd ever seen, brown cowboy boots, a blue striped cotton shirt, a cool beard, a battered leather Gladstone bag and a tobacco pouch. I swear he did his rollies with one hand. He must have been all of 19 at the time. I had not a whisker of a chance with any of the girls in the hostel. Life just ain't fair. And to make matters even worse, as well as being so cool he was also very nice and introduced me to churros with chocolate sauce. You had to be up sort of early for a 19-year-old to get the first of the day when the oil was clean and fresh. But I never forgot them, any more than I forgot about him. You don't, do you? *Serves 4*

REAL HOT CHOCOLATE
WITH CINNAMON CHURROS
CATALONIA

For the churros
Sunflower oil, for deep-frying
100 g plain flour
150 ml full-cream milk
2 medium eggs, beaten
50 g golden caster sugar
¾ teaspoon ground cinnamon

For the hot chocolate
225 g good quality plain chocolate,
  with at least 60% cocoa solids
200 ml full-cream milk

For the churros, heat some oil for deep-frying to 190°C and preheat the oven to 150°C/Gas Mark 3.

Sift the flour onto a creased sheet of greaseproof paper and set to one side. Bring the milk and 150 ml water to the boil in a pan, take the pan off the heat and add the flour all at once, beating vigorously with a wooden spoon until the mixture forms a thick paste – but don't worry about any small lumps. Leave to cool slightly and then gradually beat in enough of the eggs to make a smooth but still stiff, glossy mixture that drops reluctantly off the wooden spoon. Spoon the mixture into a piping bag fitted with a large star nozzle.

Hold the bag over the hot oil and gently squeeze out a few 10-cm lengths of the mixture. Leave them to fry for 4 minutes, turning them over halfway through, until crisp and richly golden brown. Lift them out with a slotted spoon onto a baking tray lined with lots of kitchen paper and keep warm in the oven while you cook the remainder.

For the hot chocolate, break the chocolate into a heatproof bowl and rest it over a pan containing about 2.5 cm just-simmering water. Leave until completely melted. Bring the milk to the boil in a small pan. Remove the bowl of chocolate from the heat and whisk in the hot milk. Pour into tall, narrow pots.

Mix the caster sugar and cinnamon together in a shallow dish, add the churros a few at a time, and toss them gently until lightly coated. Pile alongside each pot of hot chocolate and serve while still warm.

TO BE ACCURATE I suppose this cake should be known as Margie Agostini's orange cake. It was her signature dish at her greatly missed Caffé Agostini in Woollahra in Sydney. It seemed to me to be just made for Sicilian oranges. The recipe came from an article in the *Times* by Jill Dupleix, although I had eaten the cake at the café a few years earlier and I thought it was amazing. As Jill says, it has to be the richest, moistest, butteriest and yet lightest orange cake in the world. *Makes 1 x 22-cm cake, to serve about 8*

SICILIAN ORANGE CAKE
SICILY

250 g lightly salted butter, at room temperature, plus extra for greasing

250 g caster sugar

4 medium eggs

1½ teaspoons finely grated orange zest

250 g self-raising flour

85 ml freshly squeezed orange juice

For the icing

125 g icing sugar

5 teaspoons freshly squeezed orange juice

Preheat the oven to 170°C/Gas Mark 3. Grease and line a 22-cm clip-sided round cake tin with non-stick baking paper.

Using an electric whisk, cream the butter and sugar together for 4–5 minutes until very pale. Beat in the eggs, one at a time, beating very well between each one, if necessary adding a spoonful of flour with the last egg to prevent the mixture from curdling. Beat in the orange zest. Add the flour all at once and mix in well, then slowly mix in the orange juice.

Spoon the mixture into the prepared tin and bake on the middle shelf of the oven for 45–50 minutes or until a skewer, inserted into the centre of the cake, comes out clean. If it starts to brown too quickly, cover loosely with a sheet of lightly buttered foil.

Leave the cake, in its tin, to cool on a wire rack, then carefully remove the sides and base of the tin and peel off the paper. Put it onto a serving plate.

For the icing, sift the icing sugar into a bowl and stir in the orange juice until you have a spreadable consistency. Spread it over the top of the cake, letting it drip down the sides, and leave to set. Serve cut into slices, and store any leftovers in an airtight container.

THE MEDITERRANEAN LARDER:

INGREDIENTS SAUCES RELISHES AND BASICS

THE CORNERSTONES OF
MEDITERRANEAN COOKING

Corsica

KEY MEDITERRANEAN INGREDIENTS

Among the most exciting things I found travelling the Mediterranean over the last couple of years have been the local ingredients that give the food its characteristic flavour. The lardy, pimentón-flavoured sobrasada in Majorca; strattu, the sun-dried tomato paste of Sicily; aci biber salcasi, the hot red-pepper paste from the markets of Gaziantep and Adana in eastern Turkey; figatellu, the smoked pig's liver and clove sausage from Corsica; ras el hanout, the Moroccan spice mix – all these and more are a source of delight to the travelling cook.

SPAIN AND MALLORCA

Harina de trigo (especial para freír)
A special type of Spanish flour reserved for deep-frying, fish and seafood in particular. It is a little coarser than the usual flour, and gives the food a lighter, drier, crisper finish. Fine-ground semolina will give a similar result.

Pimentón
Paprika is the name of the famous spice from Hungary, a bright red pepper made from the sun-dried and finely ground flesh of a specific variety of red pepper, but an almost identical product is produced in Spain, where it is known as pimentón. It comes in varying degrees of pungency, from mildly sweet (dulce) through to slightly spicy (picante). Smoked pimentón, unique to Spain, has been made from peppers that have been slowly dried over oak fires instead of in the sun, and comes in three flavours – sweet, bittersweet and hot. The La Vera region of Extremadura produces a particularly high quality smoked pimentón, which was the world's first pepper spice to be given a Denominación de Origen (DO) status. I recommend the brand called La Chinata.

Bacalao (bacallá in Catalan)
This is cod, usually from Iceland or Norway, which has been salted and then partially dried, a means of preserving it that gives it a unique flavour and texture. It is popular all over the European side of the Mediterranean, particularly Spain, and especially in Catalonia. Before use, it should be soaked in numerous changes of fresh cold water over a period of about 48 hours. To check whether it has been sufficiently desalted, simply taste a small piece. I prefer to use the boneless, skinless strips of fillet, which require less preparation than other varieties.

Chorizo
This is a coarsely ground pork sausage flavoured with pimentón (see above), black pepper and garlic and, for the hotter ones (picante), chilli. Chorizo sometimes comes as a soft sausage to be cooked, typically with beans, but more commonly as a hard, cured, salami-style of sausage, which can be thinly sliced and eaten cold or used as an ingredient.

Saffron
Spain is the premier producer of saffron, and the best in the world comes from La Mancha. Saffron consists of the dried stigmas of a special variety of crocus. The flower is harvested by hand, and each one yields three stigmas. As it takes over 13,000 stigmas to make one ounce of saffron, it is easy to see why it is the most expensive and highly prized spice in the world. La Mancha saffron is deep-red in colour (other saffron is more orange or yellow) and is sold in stamen(strand) or powdered form. I prefer the strands: they have a fresher flavour. Use sparingly; otherwise it is overpowering and leaves behind a slightly 'medicinal' tint.

Arroz calasparra
Spain produces vast quantities of rice every year, most of it in the Valencia region, but a tiny amount of a special type of short-grain rice called Sollana is produced in the village of Calasparra in Murcia, and it is one of only three types of rice to be awarded the coveted Denominación de Origen (DO) status. Its plump grains absorb water and flavour while remaining firm, which makes it one of the best types of rice for paella. Bomba rice (see below) is also excellent.

Spanish hams
Spanish iberico and serrano hams are air-dried, similar to Italian parma or French bayonne hams. There is some confusion about the difference between iberico and serrano. The finest of all Spanish hams is the iberico from the pata negra pig. The four major quality categories are: (a) Jamon Iberico de Bellota, from free-range pata negra pigs fed on acorns only; (b) Jamon Iberico de Recebo, from pata negra pigs fed on acorns and other food; (c) Jamon Iberico, simply pata negra pigs fed on a nything; and (d) Jamon Serrano, ham from the large white, landrace or Belgian white pigs. Jamon de Jabugo is one of the best types of serrano ham.

Judión beans
One of the best-tasting beans in the world. They are extra large, dried white butter beans from the León region, which, once soaked, measure almost 5 cm across. They have a mild, slightly nutty flavour and firm texture, and hold their shape beautifully once cooked.

Bomba rice
Another fine quality short-grain rice grown in Spain, which has the impressive ability to absorb large quantities of liquid and thus the flavour of other ingredients. It can swell up to three times its size, but even

under extended cooking it never becomes sticky or mushy. The grains remain separate, yet still moist and firm: one of the desired features of a good paella.

Sobrasada

This is a Mallorcan speciality, a soft, red, almost paté-like cured pork sausage, flavoured with garlic and pimentón. It is often eaten simply spread on bread, but it is also great in cooking because of its melting quality. It comes in two varieties: spicy (tied with a red string) and mild (tied with white string). As I write, not yet available in the UK, but I'm working on it! Instead, use chorizo.

ITALY, SICILY AND SARDINIA

Peperoncino

This is a sweet but fiercely hot type of dried red chilli, which comes whole or in flakes. Widely available in supermarkets as crushed dried chillies.

Dried skinned and split broad beans: fave sgusciate

Dried broad beans are popular all over the Mediterranean and the Middle East. They come in two forms: as whole beans, dried with their skins on, which are brown in colour, rather than green as one might expect; and as skinned and split beans, which are creamy in colour. The creamy-coloured beans are the ones I have used for the recipes in this book.

CHEESE
Fresh ricotta

This is made from the whey left over from making ewe's or cow's milk cheeses, rather than whole milk. As the name ricotta ('recooked') suggests, the whey, which still contains some protein and fat, is reheated with a few crystals of citric acid so that small clumps of protein form. These float to the surface and are skimmed off and left to drain in 20-cm-wide wicker baskets (though more often than not now these are made out of plastic), then cooled rapidly. Because of its high moisture content, ricotta should be eaten within a few days of being purchased – best of all, a day after it was made. More than a few days and it starts to yellow and become bitter and sharp, and is no longer good for eating.

Ricotta salata

This is one of Italy's more unusual cheeses. The milk curds, made as for fresh ricotta, are lightly salted, pressed and dried and then aged for at least three months, producing a rindless, pure white cheese with a dense, spongy texture much like feta. The flavour is mild and nutty yet sweet, and the cheese is particularly good crumbled or grated over pasta or garlicky sautéed vegetables, tomato sauces and bean dishes.

Provolone

Provolone is a 'stretched-curd' cheese made from cow's milk and comes in two forms: sweet (*dolce*) and hot (*piccante*). Provolone dolce is made using calf's

rennet and is aged for only two months. It has a thin, waxed rind, a mild, delicate flavour and smooth, silky texture; it is ideal as a table cheese, and becomes stringy when cooked. Provolone piccante is made using goat's or lamb's rennet for a spicier, stronger flavour, and is aged for an average of 12 months to produce a harder cheese, darker in colour and with a tough rind. This is ideal at the end of a meal or for cooking or for grating over pasta.

Taleggio

This is a square-shaped, rich and creamy, semi-soft cheese with a thin rosy-brown rind and rich, buttery centre. The rind should not be removed before use as this is where taleggio's most intense flavour is to be found. A perfectly ripe cheese should be slightly runny nearer the crust and slightly firmer in the centre, with a fragrantly sweet yet pungent flavour. It is wonderful eaten as it is with fresh bread, lettuce salads or fresh fruit, or cooked, as in my recipe for *Parmigiana di melanzana* on page 79.

Pecorino sardo

This cheese is made on the island of Sardinia from the milk of their indigenous sheep and comes in two forms. *Dolce* is aged for between 20 and 60 days and has a delicate, sweet flavour and supple texture, and *maturo* is matured for up to 12 months to produce a hard, dry, granular cheese with a sharp salty tang, which is ideal grated over pasta or vegetable dishes.

MEAT
Pancetta

Pancetta is a fundamental ingredient in Italian cuisine. It is salted and cured belly of pork, much like our streaky bacon, which can be left as it is, flavoured with herbs, smoked or aged. It comes either as a rolled joint or flat, like a side of bacon, with the fat along one side.

Napoli salami

This pork and beef sausage is flavoured with red and black pepper and then lightly smoked and cured for two months to produce a wonderfully sharp, spicy salami.

Prosciutto

This is the general name given to the salt-cured hams of Italy, which are air-dried for up to two years (during which time they lose up to 30 per cent of their original weight) to produce a ham that is sweet and slightly nutty in flavour and dry in texture. Two well-known varieties are Prosciutto di Parma and Prosciutto di San Danielle.

Luganega

This is a traditional raw pork sausage from the Lombardy region in the north of Italy, made from 100 per cent meat (and no filler), with a hint of garlic and fennel seeds. Those from Monza, a suburb of Milan and the scene of the Grand Prix, are said to be among the best. It comes as one long, thin (chipolata-sized) unlinked sausage, which can be crumbled for making pasta sauces, or fried and grilled.

Risotto rice

This includes arborio and carnaroli, as well as maratelli, roma and vialone. Most rice labelled as risotto rice is arborio. As with many ingredients, you will get a better quality if you pay that bit more. Risotto rice is a short-grain rice, essential for making the dish. Do not rinse this rice before cooking, as the layer of starch coating the grains will give the rice its creamy texture. Constantly stirring the rice during cooking

allows the grains to swell and absorb liquid at a steady rate, but also encourages the outside of the grains to break down, thickening some of the liquid and giving the finished dish its classic creamy texture, while still leaving the grains subtly firm at the centre. Carnaroli is the variety favoured by restaurant cooks because it keeps its bite for a little longer – a bit more forgiving if you neglect the pan for a minute or two.

Pasta

The Italians use the dried variety more than they use fresh pasta. There are a few brands I recommend – such as De Cecco, Agnesi or Voiello – although most supermarket pasta is perfectly acceptable. Some of the shapes used in the recipes in this book are less common than the spaghetti, linguine or tagliatelle we are all familiar with. Here is a quick run-down:

Ditali – taking its name from the Italian for 'thimble', this is a small, very short macaroni-shaped pasta about 5 mm long and 5 mm in diameter.

Gnocchetti sardi – also known as *malloreddus*, a small, shell-shaped pasta made to look like the popular fresh potato dumplings called gnocchi. A speciality of Sardinia; sometimes flavoured with saffron.

Orecchiette – a slightly thicker, more rustic small pasta, shaped like little bowls, or indeed 'little ears'. Often made from fresh pasta, as well as available dried. A speciality of Puglia.

Orzo – meaning 'barley', this small pasta, shaped like a large grain of rice, is also known as *puntaletta* or *grano*. Traditionally used in soups and stews but also great as a side dish or in salads.

Rigatoni – a medium-sized tubular pasta, slightly shorter than tortiglioni (see below), and with straight ridges on the outside; perfect for the *Beef and macaroni pie* on page 136.

Tortiglioni – a medium-sized tubular pasta with spiralled ridges on the outside. Ideal

for baking, as in the *Beef and macaroni pie* on page 136.

Tubetti – similar to *ziti* (below) but cut into slightly shorter lengths.

Ziti – a medium-sized tubular pasta, slightly curved and with a smooth surface.

Capers

The matured but unopened flower buds of a Mediterranean bramble-like shrub, *Capparis spinosa*, which grows all over Italy. Those from Sicily, and especially Pantelleria, a tiny volcanic island a few miles off the Sicilian coast, are considered to be Italy's best. The flower buds are picked every eight to ten days from mid-May to August, when they are in their infancy and at the peak of flavour. They are then washed and jarred in sea salt to retain their unique flavour and texture. (Capers are also preserved in vinegar or brine but they lose some of their flavour and texture to the liquid, and the flavour of those in vinegar is overpowered.) Salted capers just need to be rinsed and soaked in cold water for about 15 minutes, rinsed and soaked again before using.

Strattu

A sun-dried tomato paste unique to the island of Sicily. Ripe tomatoes are juiced, seeded and cooked with salt for about an hour, then passed through a food mill. The resulting purée is spread onto large wooden boards or tabletops and left in the sun to dry for 4 to 5 days, stirred every once in a while, until all the moisture has evaporated, leaving a dark red paste with a texture like putty. During this process an amazing 20 kg of tomatoes is reduced to 1 kg, giving it a highly concentrated flavour. It is softened in a little hot water for cooking. Use it as you would use regular tomato purée, bearing in mind that it's much more intense. Sadly unavailable in this country, but who knows? I might be able to rectify that.

Cavalo nero

An Italian cabbage with long, dark inky-green leaves and a good, strong flavour.

Just strip the leaves of their tough stalks before using, unless the vegetable is very young. Perfect for all recipes that use cabbage but particularly good sautéed in olive oil with just a little chopped garlic and crushed dried chilli.

Anchovies

These come either salted or preserved in oil; of those preserved in oil, some are in olive oil and some in vegetable oil. For all the recipes in this book I use anchovies in olive oil, and nothing else. Check the tin before you buy: not every tin is the same. Generally speaking, the more you pay, the better the quality.

Bottarga muggine

Sometimes called 'poor man's caviar', this is the dried, salted roe of the grey mullet, covered in a thin layer of wax to prevent further drying and to inhibit exposure to light. It is a speciality of Sicily and Sardinia (and Greece). Other varieties are made from the roe of tuna or swordfish, but neither is quite as good as that from the grey mullet. It is relatively expensive but you don't need much. It has a strong, concentrated sea flavour and is wonderful simply finely grated over cooked pasta (see page 106).

Torrone

Torrone, otherwise known as nougat (and turrón in Spain), is a sweet made from honey, well-whipped egg whites, vanilla and – usually – almonds, but sometimes pistachios, walnuts or hazelnuts, shaped into a block or a round cake. It comes in two varieties, hard and soft. It is the hard, brittle variety you need for the semi-freddo on page 185. Good examples come from Sicily and Sardinia; sold in good supermarkets or Italian delicatessens.

Savoiardi

These are crisp, golden brown, delicately flavoured fingers of sponge cake, which get their name from the area where they were supposedly invented, the Aosta valley in northern Italy, running from the Po valley to Mont Blanc, once part of the Duchy of Savoy. Preparing them properly requires skill and flair so most Italian housewives are content to buy them. They are not dissimilar to sponge fingers but are slightly thicker with a far superior texture and taste. As they are they make a wonderful accompaniment to ice cream or zabaglione, but they are also used extensively in desserts, such as tiramisu. They need to be crisp and fresh so buy them only when you need to use them.

Vin santo

This is a dark, amber-coloured, very sweet dessert wine from Tuscany, made from grapes that have been left on the vines, then laid out on straw mats to partly dry and concentrate their juice to a raisiny syrup. The drink's name, 'holy wine', is said to arise from a priestly fondness for the stuff. It is traditionally served with rock-hard vanilla-flavoured almond or hazelnut biscuits, the trick being to dip them into the wine to soften them before eating. However, it is also good in the making of other desserts, such as zabaglione.

Marsala

Italian fortified wine, produced in the region surrounding the city of Marsala in Sicily. Rich and amber-coloured, ranges from the dry, unsweetened marsala vergine to the toffee-sweet marsala superiore.

CORSICA

Figatellu

The name of this famous, lightly smoked, U-shaped liver sausage from Corsica comes from *fegato*, the Italian for liver. It is found in different guises, often flavoured with garlic, red wine, and sometimes herbs. After one and a half or two weeks curing and drying in well-ventilated sheds it is ready to be cooked, traditionally over the grill or open fire, and served with fried eggs and chestnut pulenda, a type of polenta made from chestnut flour. After two to three months it becomes much harder and can be eaten raw.

GREECE

Orzo

The rice-shaped pasta is known all over Greece as *kritharaki* and is often served in salads or as a side dish to lamb, beef or chicken dishes.

Feta

Many other countries, particularly Denmark, were once allowed to produce their own version of feta, but it is now a protected designation of origin (PDO) cheese, which limits the name, at least in the EU, to Greek feta. This is a firm, fresh, white cheese with a soft crumbly texture and salty herbaceous flavour, made from goat's or ewe's milk. Once drained, the cheese is cut into slices, salted and 'pickled' in vast tins or plastic containers, covered with a mixture of brine and whey.

Kefalotiri

Kefalotiri is a dry, firm, ewe's milk cheese from Greece, full of irregular holes, which ranges in colour from white through to pale yellow, depending on the grazing of the sheep. It is a fresh, slightly sharp-tasting, quite salty cheese with a distinct flavour of ewe's milk. However, it's not easy to come by, so use Italian Parmesan instead.

Greek oregano

Oregano is native to the Mediterranean region, though it can now be found all over the world in various forms, often confusingly called marjoram, rather than oregano. However, in my opinion, nothing has the flavour of Greek oregano, *Origanum vulgare*. This herb has round, pale green, hairy leaves, with knots of tiny white flowers, and a very aromatic, strong flavour, which is one of the cornerstones of all Greek cuisine. This herb takes well to drying, but do try to buy it still on the branch, so to speak, not in powdered form in small jars.

TURKEY

Aleppo pepper

A finely ground (though not powdered) red chilli from eastern Turkey and northern Syria. It is made from a moderately hot red chilli that is sun-dried, seeded, then finely crushed and mixed with a few drops of oil. It is also known as Halaby pepper, Halab pepper or Near-eastern pepper, and gives an authentic Mediterranean flavour

that is pleasantly spicy but not overly hot. Cayenne is a possible substitute but it's hotter so use less.

Zahtar

Zahtar (also spelt zahter, za'atar or zatar) is a dry spice mixture based around sesame seeds, sumac and dried thyme, but all over the eastern Mediterranean and North Africa the combination of seeds and spices differs. In eastern Turkey the one I came across was a mixture of dry-roasted and ground sesame seeds, chickpeas, pistachios and watermelon seeds, together with ground cumin, paprika, fennel seed, dried thyme, sumac powder and salt. Not only is it used in marinades or to flavour grilled meats, but it is also popular as a dry dip, along with some olive oil, for bread, especially at breakfast time.

Tahini (tahina)

This a thick, Middle-Eastern paste made from ground hulled and lightly roasted sesame seeds, and is a major ingredient in dishes such as hummus and baba ghanoush (moutabal). There are two types of tahini: the light, ivory-coloured one is superior in taste and texture to the darker one.

Bulgar wheat

Also known as bulgur, burghul or cracked wheat, this staple of the Mediterranean kitchen since ancient times is produced by par-boiling wheat, drying it once more, then coarsely grinding it to crack the grains and remove the outer layers of bran. It is then steamed or boiled in numerous ways for eating and is highly nutritious, with a pleasing and distinctive nutty taste and flavour.

MOROCCO

Harissa

This is a fiery hot, deep-red pepper paste from North Africa, made from chillies, red pepper, tomato, saffron, coriander, cayenne, sometimes cumin and caraway, and salt, and it can be used as a condiment or as an ingredient in cooking. One well-known variety, known as rose harissa, also contains rose petals. It is sold in tubes, cans and jars, but is easy to make yourself (see my recipe on the facing page).

Ras el hanout

A unique blend of herbs and spices used across North Africa. The Arabic name is 'top of the shop': meaning it's a mixture of the best spices the shop has to offer. In the Moroccan souks (markets) it is a great honour to have the most sought-after blend, and it is commonly thought of as an aphrodisiac. But there is no set combination of spices that makes up ras el hanout. Most contain over a dozen different spices and often as many as thirty. Typical ingredients include cardamom, mace, nutmeg, cinnamon, chilli, cumin, coriander, black pepper, white pepper, ginger, cloves, allspice, turmeric and saffron. More unusual additions are rosebuds, anise, orris root, lavender and galangal. Ras el hanout gives a golden colour and an aromatic and enticing flavour to dishes and is often used in tagines and b'stilla, or stirred into couscous and rice.

Preserved lemons

These are lemons that have been pickled in salt and their own juices; they add a distinctive salty-sweet flavour to a wide variety of North African dishes. The softened rind is separated from the flesh, finely chopped and added at the end of cooking, whereas the flesh is generally either blended with the sauce or discarded. They are very easy to make at home (see my recipe on the facing page).

Couscous

Couscous is made of minute, roughly spherical granules of moistened semolina wheat, a type of durum wheat, coated in finely ground wheat flour. Traditional hand-made couscous takes a considerable amount of time to prepare, but now ready prepared, pre-steamed and dried couscous is available, which takes only minutes to cook. It is a staple food of Eastern Morocco, Tunisia, Libya and Algeria, and is also popular in southern France and Sicily. It is nutritious, much like pasta, and is traditionally served with meat and vegetable stews.

Orange flower water

Oranges proliferate across the Mediterranean, where even their blossoms are distilled into a clear flower water. This is popular in Middle Eastern and North African cooking, where it lends a unique, slightly perfumed flavour to many desserts, pastries and cakes. A similar product is distilled from rose petals.

Dried skinned and split broad beans

All types of dried beans and pulses are widely used in Morocco, especially these broad beans (see also page 205), which are skinned and split before drying. They feature in the famous soup called bessara (see my recipe on page 179).

ESSENTIAL TECHNIQUES AND BASIC RECIPES

How to prepare globe artichokes

For artichoke bases: Break off the stems close to the base of each globe and discard. Now cut off the leafy top half of each globe and bend back the remaining green leaves, letting them snap off close to the base, until you reach the pale, softer leaves and the hairy choke at the centre. Pull away the soft leaves, then slice away the choke from the base with a small knife, or scrape it away with a teaspoon. Neatly trim away the remaining dark green bottoms of the leaves from the underside to leave a convex-shaped base. Drop the artichoke bases into a pan of acidulated water (water and plenty of lemon juice) as you go, to prevent them from discolouring. You need larger globes to prepare bases from.

For artichoke hearts: Trim down the stems of each globe to about 4–5 cm and then cut each one lengthways through the stem into quarters. Cut away the hairy choke from the centre of each quarter with a small, sharp knife. Now turn each quarter over and bend back the darker green leaves, letting them snap off close to the base of each leaf but making sure you leave behind the fleshy part, until you start to reach the paler green leaves in the centre. Slice the top half of the remaining leaves away. Drop the hearts into a bowl of acidulated water (water and plenty of lemon juice) as you go, to prevent them from discolouring. You can prepare hearts from any size of globe, but the fresher the better.

Roasted red peppers

Either: Spear the stalk end on a fork and turn the pepper in the flame of a gas burner or blowtorch until the skin has blistered and blackened.

Or: Roast the pepper in the oven preheated to 220°C/Gas Mark 7 for 20–25 minutes, turning once until the skin is black.

Then: Remove the pepper from the oven and leave to cool. Break it in half and remove the stalk, skin and seeds. The flesh is now ready to use.

Turkish red pepper paste (Aci biber salcasi)

This isn't identical to what is available in the local markets, which is sun-dried, but it does lend a good, concentrated red-pepper flavour to Turkish dishes, such as the recipe for bulgar pilaf on page 174. If you live in London, however, you should be able to get the sun-dried paste from Turkish grocers in places like Dalston and Hackney.

Makes about 175g
4 large red peppers
1–4 medium-hot red chillies (depending on how hot you want your finished paste to be)
4 teaspoons olive oil
1 teaspoon caster sugar
1 teaspoon salt

Cut the red peppers into quarters and discard the stalks and seeds. Cut the chillies in half, trim away the stalks and, for a milder paste, discard the seeds. Put the red peppers, chillies, 3 tablespoons water, olive oil, sugar and salt into a food processor and process until smooth. Transfer the mixture to a medium-sized saucepan and simmer gently for 1 hour, until the mixture has reduced to a thick paste. You will need to gradually lower the heat and stir it more often as the paste reduces and gets thicker, to prevent it from burning on the bottom of the pan. Leave to cool, then spoon into a sealable plastic container and store in the fridge for up to 1 week. Can also be frozen.

Harissa

This is a good standby to have in the fridge to stir into many North African soups or stews. This will keep in the fridge for up to a month.

Makes about 6 tablespoons
1 roasted red pepper (see above)
1 teaspoon tomato purée
1 teaspoon ground coriander
A pinch of saffron strands
2 medium-hot red chillies, stalks removed and roughly chopped
¼ teaspoon cayenne pepper
½ teaspoon salt

Put the roasted red pepper flesh, tomato purée, ground coriander, saffron, chillies, cayenne pepper and salt into a processor and blend until smooth. Transfer to a small bowl. It is now ready to use.

Salsa verde

This simple Italian sauce is often one of the best accompaniments to grilled fish and meats, especially steak.

Serves 6–8
20 g flat-leaf parsley leaves, very roughly chopped
7g mint leaves, very roughly chopped
3 tablespoons capers in brine, drained and rinsed
6 anchovy fillets in olive oil, drained
1 garlic clove
1 teaspoon Dijon mustard
1½ tablespoons lemon juice
120 ml extra virgin olive oil
½ teaspoon salt

Pile the parsley, mint, capers, anchovies and garlic onto a chopping board and chop together into a coarse paste. Transfer the mixture into a bowl and stir in the mustard, lemon juice, olive oil and salt. The sauce is now ready to use. It doesn't keep well, so use it soon after making.

Preserved lemons

This is a characteristic flavour of Morocco, and very simple to make for yourself. Just ensure the lemons are small or they won't fit into or fill the jar.

3–4 small unwaxed lemons per 500 ml Kilner jar
75 g salt per jar
Fresh lemon juice

Cut the lemons almost into quarters, leaving them attached at the stalk end.

Sprinkle as much salt as you can into the cuts, squeeze them back into shape and push into the jar, stalk-end down, packing them in tightly – they will fit with a little persuasion.

Sprinkle over the rest of the salt, seal and leave for 4–5 days, giving the jar a shake every now and then, until they have produced quite a lot of juice. Then top up the jar with lemon juice so that the lemons are completely covered. Seal and leave for a couple of weeks before using.

Charmoula

Charmoula (also spelt chermoula) is a paste made from spices and fresh herbs and is used in Moroccan, Algerian and Tunisian cooking, usually to flavour fish and seafood dishes, but also for chicken, meat and vegetable dishes. There are many different recipes, using different combinations of spices, but this is one I like the best.

Makes 175 ml

3 garlic cloves, roughly chopped
1½ teaspoons ground cumin
1½ teaspoons paprika
½ medium-hot red chilli, seeded and chopped
½ teaspoon saffron strands
Juice 1 small lemon
A small handful of coriander leaves
A small handful of mint leaves
4 tablespoons extra virgin olive oil

Put all the ingredients into the small bowl of a food processor with 1 teaspoon salt and blend to a smooth paste. (You could also make it by hand, like the salsa verde, above.) It is now ready to use. It also keeps for 3–4 days in the fridge.

Skordalia

This is designed to be served with grilled fish, poached salt cod, courgette fritters, new potatoes, crunchy fennel, boiled artichokes or indeed anything which a lovely cold sauce, sharp with garlic and tart with lemon, would enhance.

135 g floury maincrop potatoes, such as Maris Piper
15 g garlic
½ teaspoon salt
100 ml extra virgin olive oil
Juice of ½ lemon
A little warm water

Peel the potatoes, cut them into chunks and put into a pan of cold salted water

(1 teaspoon per 600 ml). Bring to the boil and leave to simmer for about 20 minutes until very soft. Drain.

Put the garlic into a mortar with the salt and pound to a paste. Add the potatoes and continue pounding with the pestle until they are smooth. Now beat in the olive oil a little at a time to build up an emulsion. As with mayonnaise, don't add it too quickly. Finally add the lemon juice, and a little water if needed to achieve the right consistency, which should be that of mayonnaise.

Pickled chillies

It's quite hard to get hold of the mild slender pale green chillies the Turks use, though you can buy them in Turkish grocers, particularly in Dalston and Hackney in London. Supermarkets in the UK have started selling the Turkish Marmara pepper, which is slightly hot. I like to pickle these with a few hotter, green finger chillies. I also tend to add some sliced carrots, cucumbers and red peppers, since often in Turkey you get a selection of pickles with your köfte or kebab.

Fills a 750-ml jar (such as Le Parfait)

350 g green chillies
30 g salt
15 g sugar
1 teaspoon pickling spices
400 ml white wine or cider vinegar

Remove the stalks from the chillies. Boil a pan of water and immerse the chillies for 2 minutes. Remove, drain, turn into a bowl of cold water and drain again.

Bring the salt, sugar, pickling spices and wine or vinegar to the boil and simmer for 2 minutes.

Pack the chillies into the jar or container, pour on the vinegar mixture and top up with a little more vinegar if necessary. Refrigerate and keep for at least 24 hours before using.

Clarified butter

Place butter in a small pan and leave it over a very low heat until it has melted. Skim off any scum from the surface and pour off the clear (clarified) butter into a bowl, leaving behind the milky white

solids that will have settled on the bottom of the pan. The butter is ready to use.

Dried white breadcrumbs

Process crustless white bread in a food processor into crumbs. Spread onto a large baking tray and bake at 140°C/Gas Mark 1 for 20 minutes. Remove, turn the crumbs over and return to the oven for a further 15–20 minutes until crisp and dry but not browned. Leave to cool and then store in an airtight container; they keep very well.

Fresh egg pasta

Makes about 250 g

225 g plain flour
1½ teaspoons extra virgin olive oil
4 medium egg yolks
2 medium eggs
½ teaspoon salt

Put all the ingredients into a food processor and blend until they come together into a dough. Tip out onto a work surface and knead for about 10 minutes until smooth and elastic. Wrap in clingfilm and leave to rest for 10–15 minutes before rolling and using as the recipe instructs.

Flatbreads

Makes 8

350 g plain flour
1 teaspoon salt
2 teaspoons easy-blend yeast
2 tablespoons extra virgin olive oil

For the flatbreads, sift the flour, salt and yeast into a bowl and make a well in the centre. Add 250 ml warm water and the olive oil and mix together to make a soft dough. Transfer to a lightly floured surface and knead for 5 minutes. Put back into the bowl, cover and leave somewhere warm for about 1 hour until doubled in size.

Punch back the dough, turn it out onto a lightly floured surface and knead once more until smooth. Divide into 8 pieces and roll each one into a ball. Cover and leave to rise for 10 minutes.

Meanwhile, preheat the oven to 240°C/ Gas Mark 9. Working with one ball of dough at a time, roll it out flat until it is about 22 cm across. Place it on a greased baking sheet, spray lightly with a little water and bake for 2 minutes. Check to see that it hasn't gone hard and, if not, cook for about 1 minute more. You want it to be cooked through and still pliable, not hard or browned. Remove, wrap in a tea towel and keep warm. Repeat for the rest of the breads.

Vegetable stock

2 large onions
2 large carrots
1 head celery
1 bulb fennel
1 bulb garlic
3 bay leaves
1 teaspoon salt
3 litres water

Slice all the vegetables (you don't need to peel the garlic), put into a saucepan with the water, bring to the boil and simmer for 1 hour. Strain and use.

Chicken stock
Use the bones from a roasted chicken for a slightly deeper-flavoured stock.

Makes about 1.75 litres
Bones from a 1.5-kg uncooked chicken, or 450 g chicken wings or drumsticks
1 large carrot, chopped
2 celery sticks, sliced
2 leeks, cleaned and sliced
2 fresh or dried bay leaves
2 thyme sprigs
2.25 litres water

Put all the ingredients into a large pan and bring just to the boil, skimming off any scum from the surface as it appears. Leave to simmer very gently for 2 hours – it is important not to let it boil as this will force the fat from even the leanest chicken and make the stock cloudy. Strain the stock through a sieve and leave to simmer a little longer to concentrate in flavour if necessary, then use as required. If not using immediately, leave to cool, then chill and refrigerate or freeze for later use.

Beef stock

Makes about 2.4 litres
2 tablespoons sunflower oil (optional)
2 celery sticks
2 carrots
2 onions
900 g shin of beef
5 litres water
2 bay leaves
2 thyme sprigs
1 tablespoon salt

For a pale brown stock, put all the ingredients except for the bay leaves, thyme sprigs and salt, into a large saucepan, and bring to the boil, skimming off any scum as it rises to the surface. Reduce the heat and leave to simmer for 2½ hours, adding the salt and herbs 15 minutes before the end.

For a deeper, richer-coloured stock, heat the sunflower oil in the pan, add the vegetables and beef and fry for 10–15 minutes until nicely browned, before adding the water, salt and herbs.

If not using immediately, leave to cool, then chill and refrigerate or freeze for later use.

Tomato sauce
You can make this sauce with fresh or canned tomatoes. If using fresh, make sure they have a good deep-red colour and are really juicy and with lots of flavour. Unfortunately, good tomatoes are not always easy to come by in this country. If you cannot get really good fresh tomatoes, using canned ones will give you a much better sauce.

Makes about 600 ml
6 tablespoons extra virgin olive oil
20 g garlic cloves, finely chopped
1 kg well-flavoured tomatoes, skinned, or
  2 x 400-g cans plum tomatoes
Salt and freshly ground black pepper

Put the olive oil and garlic into a medium-sized pan and as soon as the garlic starts to sizzle, add the tomatoes and simmer for 15–20 minutes, breaking up the tomatoes with a wooden spoon as they cook, until the sauce has reduced and thickened.

Season with 1 teaspoon salt and some freshly ground black pepper. The sauce is ready to use. If not using immediately, leave to cool, then chill and refrigerate or freeze for later use.

Beurre manié
Blend equal quantities of softened butter and plain flour together into a smooth paste. Cover and keep in the fridge; it will keep as for butter.

Mayonnaise
This recipe includes instructions for making mayonnaise in the liquidizer or by hand. When made mechanically you use a whole egg and the result is lighter, while mayonnaise made by hand is softer and richer. You can use either sunflower oil, olive oil or a mixture of the two. It will keep in the fridge for up to 1 week.

Makes 300 ml
1 egg or 2 egg yolks
2 teaspoons white wine vinegar
½ teaspoon salt
1 tablespoon mustard (optional)
300 ml sunflower oil or olive oil

To make the mayonnaise by hand: Make sure all the ingredients are at room temperature before you start. Put the egg yolks, vinegar, salt and mustard if using into a mixing bowl and then rest the bowl on a cloth to stop it slipping. Using a wire whisk, first lightly break the yolks. Then gradually beat the oil into the egg mixture, a few drops at a time, until you have incorporated it all. Once you have added the same volume of oil as the original mixture of egg yolks and vinegar, you can add the remaining oil a little more quickly.

To make the mayonnaise in a machine: Put the whole egg, vinegar, salt and mustard if using into a liquidizer or food processor. Turn on the machine and then slowly add the oil through the hole in the lid until you have a thick emulsion.

Allioli
This is a punchy garlic sauce from Catalonia. I first had it on board a fishing

boat stirred into a fish stew but they also use it as a dip with tapas or as a sauce for grilled fish and rice dishes.

Makes about 175 ml
4 garlic cloves, peeled
½ teaspoon salt
1 medium egg yolk
175 ml extra virgin olive oil

Put the garlic cloves onto a chopping board and crush them under the blade of a large knife. Sprinkle them with the salt and then work them with the knife blade into a smooth paste. Scrape the garlic paste into a bowl and add the egg yolk. Using an electric mixer, whisk everything together, and then very gradually whisk in the olive oil to make a thick mayonnaise-like mixture.

WHERE TO GET INGREDIENTS

SPANISH

For bacalao (salt cod), dried Judión butter beans, harina de trigo, arroz calasparra (paella rice), chorizo, paprika and other Spanish ingredients:

Brindisa
Floral Hall
Stoney Street
Borough Market
London SE1
Tel: 020 7407 1036

Brindisa
32 Exmouth Market
Clerkenwell
London
EC1R 4QE
Tel: 020 7713 1666

If you do not live in London and it is not possible to visit the retail outlets above, please call the Borough Market stall for stockists in your area.
www.purespain.co.uk for arroz calasparra (paella rice) and other Spanish ingredients.
www.donquijoteltd.com for bacalao (salt cod) and other Spanish ingredients.

www.sayellfoods.com for a wide variety of Spanish foods, including harina de trigo.

ITALIAN & SICILIAN

www.valvonacrolla-online.co.uk or telephone 0131 556 6066 for a wide range of mail-order Italian ingredients including canned San Marzano plum tomatoes
www.camisa.co.uk for Italian ingredients such as cheeses, pasta, charcuterie including smoked pancetta and rice. Telephone 01992 763076 to order fresh luganega sausages.
www.nifeislife.com for dried skinned and split broad beans (fave sgusciate) and other dried beans and pulses, pecorino sardo maturo, ricotta salata and a wide range of other cheeses, pasta, rice, charcuterie, and other Italian ingredients.

SARDINIAN

www.vallebona.co.uk for pecorino sardo maturo and other Sardinian cheeses, fresh sausages with fennel seeds (similar to luganega), bottarga muggine (salted grey mullet roe), black squid ink, small pantelleria capers, carnaroli risotto rice, anchovies, smoked pancetta and other Italian charcuterie, pasta and other ingredients.
www.thespiceshop.co.uk for peperoncino and other spices

GREEK

Contact Odysea on 020 7796 1166 or **www.odysea.com** for Greek ingredients such as kefalotiri and feta cheese, 'gigandes' (giant butter beans), rice, olives, etc. Greek Connection have a stall in Borough Market (see address above) selling Greek cheeses and olives etc.

TURKISH

www.thespiceshop.co.uk for Aleppo red pepper flakes and a wide range of other spices and herbs.
www.seasonedpioneers.co.uk for zahtar, plus smoked paprika, saffron and many other spices and spice blends.

MOROCCAN

www.maroque.co.uk for orange flower and rose water, preserved lemons, olives, couscous, tahini paste, harissa and other Moroccan ingredients.

SUPERMARKETS

Sainsbury's sell a wide variety of specialist ingredients including cooked Judión beans in jars, pomegranate molasses, paella rice and saffron.

Waitrose also sell a wide selection of unusual ingredients.

STEIN'S DELI

We stock the unusual ingredients used in this book. Visit **www.rickstein.com/onlineshop** or telephone 01841 533250 for mail order enquiries.

NOTES ON THE RECIPES

• All teaspoon and tablespoon measurements are level unless otherwise stated and are based on measuring spoons, where 1 teaspoon = 5 ml and 1 tablespoon = 15 ml. Don't be tempted to use a coffee spoon or an old-fashioned serving-size tablespoon instead.

• All cooking times are approximate.

• All recipes have been tested in a conventional oven. If you have fan oven, you will probably need to adjust the dial by about 20°C. So for 200°C, set the dial at about 180°C. I always keep an oven thermometer hanging from one of the racks so that I can check the temperature before I start cooking.

• Free-range eggs and chickens are always recommended.

• Recipes made with raw or lightly cooked eggs should be avoided by anyone who is pregnant or in a vulnerable health group.

• Exact cooking times for pasta and soaked dried beans vary according to the brand and age of the ingredients.

• If you like to be precise about garlic quantities, work on the basis that an average clove weighs 6 g.

CONVERSION CHARTS

LIQUID MEASURES

15 ml	½ fl oz
20 ml	¾ fl oz
25 ml	1 fl oz
35 ml	1¼ fl oz
40 ml	1½ fl oz
50 ml	2 fl oz
60 ml	2¼ fl oz
65 ml	2½ fl oz
85 ml	3 fl oz
100 ml	3½ fl oz
120 ml	4 fl oz
150 ml	5 fl oz (¼ pint)
175 ml	6 fl oz
200 ml	7 fl oz
250 ml	8 fl oz
275 ml	9 fl oz
300 ml	10 fl oz (½ pint)
325 ml	11 fl oz
350 ml	12 fl oz
375 ml	13 fl oz
400 ml	14 fl oz
450 ml	15 fl oz (¾ pint)
475 ml	16 fl oz
500 ml	17 fl oz
550 ml	18 fl oz
575 ml	19 fl oz
600 ml	1 pint (20 fl oz)
750 ml	1¼ pints
900 ml	1½ pints
1 litre	1¾ pints
1.2 litres	2 pints
1.25 litres	2¼ pints
1.5 litres	2½ pints
1.6 litres	2¾ pints
1.75 litres	3 pints
2 litres	3½ pints
2.25 litres	4 pints
2.5 litres	4½ pints
2.75 litres	5 pints
3.4 litres	6 pints
3.9 litres	7 pints
4.5 litres	8 pints
5 litres	9 pints

SOLID MEASURES

5 g	⅛ oz
10 g	¼ oz
15 g	½ oz
20 g	¾ oz
25 g	1 oz
40 g	1½ oz
50 g	2 oz
65 g	2½ oz
75 g	3 oz
90 g	3½ oz
100 g	4 oz (¼ lb)
120 g	4½ oz
135 g	4¾ oz
150 g	5 oz
165 g	5½ oz
175 g	6 oz
185 g	6½ oz
200 g	7 oz
215 g	7½ oz
225 g	8 oz (½ lb)
250 g	9 oz
275 g	10 oz
300 g	11 oz
350 g	12 oz (¾ lb)
375 g	13 oz
400 g	14 oz
425 g	15 oz
450 g	1 lb (16 oz)
550 g	1¼ lb
750 g	1½ lb / 1¾ lb
1 kg	2¼ lb
1.25 kg	2½ lb / 2¾ lb
1.5 kg	3 lb / 3¼ lb / 3½ lb
1.75 kg	4 lb / 4¼ lb
2 kg	4½ lb / 4¾ lb
2.25 kg	5 lb / 5¼ lb
2.5 kg	5½ lb / 5¾ lb
2.75 kg	6 lb
3 kg	7 lb
3.5 kg	8 lb
4 kg	9 lb
4.5 kg	10 lb
5 kg	11 lb
5.5 kg	12 lb

LINEAR MEASURES

3 mm	⅛ inch
5 mm	¼ inch
1 cm	½ inch
2 cm	¾ inch
2.5 cm	1 inch
3 cm	1¼ inch
4 cm	1½ inch
4.5 cm	1¾ inch
5 cm	2 inches
6 cm	2½ inches
7.5 cm	3 inches
9 cm	3½ inches
10 cm	4 inches
13 cm	5 inches
15 cm	6 inches
18 cm	7 inches
20 cm	8 inches
23 cm	9 inches
25 cm	10 inches
28 cm	11 inches
30 cm	12 inches (1 foot)

OVEN TEMPERATURES

Gas	°C	Fan °C	°F	Oven temp.
¼	110	90	225	Very cool
½	120	100	250	Very cool
1	140	120	275	Cool or slow
2	150	130	300	Cool or slow
3	160	140	325	Warm
4	180	160	350	Moderate
5	190	170	375	Moderately hot
6	200	180	400	Fairly hot
7	220	200	425	Hot
8	230	210	450	Very hot
9	240	220	475	Very hot

INDEX

Sardinia